WITHDRAWN

Index to Stories of Hymns

AMS PRESS
NEW YORK

INDEX
to
Stories of Hymns

An analytical catalog of
twelve much-used books

by

ALICE M. RICHARDSON

Cataloger and in charge of the
Departmental Library of Religious Education,
Hartford Seminary Foundation Library.

Yardley, Penna.
F. S. COOK & SON, Inc.
1929

Library of Congress Cataloging in Publication Data

Richardson, Alice Marion.
  Index to stories of hymns.
  Sources indexed: Benson, Bonsall, Brown & Butterworth, Colson, Eggleston, Ikenberry, Morrison, Paine, Price, N. Smith, R. Smith.
  Reprint of the 1929 ed. published by F. S. Cook, Yardley, Pa.
  1. Hymns—History and criticism—Indexes. 2. Hymns, English—History and criticism—Indexes. I. Title.
ML128.H8R4   1975   783.9'09   72-1690
ISBN 0-404-09911-4

Reprinted from an original copy in the collections of the Memorial Library at the University of Wisconsin

From the edition of 1929, Yardley, Pa.
First AMS edition published in 1975
Manufactured in the United States of America

AMS PRESS INC.
NEW YORK, N.Y. 10003

PREFACE

The books included in this index are those most constantly used by the students of the Hartford School of Religious Education, and have been analyzed as a practical aid to usual reference work.

It has been suggested that the index might be of similar use in the reference work of religious education and public libraries generally and is accordingly printed as it stands without delaying for revisions.

A. M. R.

Case Memorial Library,
   Hartford Seminary Foundation,
      Hartford, Conn.
         September, 1928.

ABBREVIATIONS OF SOURCES INDEXED

Benson = Benson, Louis F. Studies of familiar hymns. 1921
Benson 2 = Benson, Louis F. Studies of familiar hymns. 2d series. 1923.
Bonsall = Bonsall, Elizabeth H. Famous hymns with stories and pictures. c.1923.
Brown = Brown & Butterworth. The story of the hymns and tunes. c1906.
Colson = Colson, Elizabeth. Hymn stories. c1925.
Eggleston = Eggleston, Margaret W. Hymn stories for children 1920.
Ikenberry = Ikenberry, Charles S. Motives and expression in religious educ. c1922
Morrison = Morrison, Duncan. The great hymns of the church. 1890.
Paine = Paine, Silas H. Stories of the great hymns of the church. c1926.
Price = Price, Carl F. One hundred and one hymn stories. c1923.
Smith N = Smith, Nicholas. Hymns historically famous. 1901.
Smith R = Smith, Robert E. Modern messages from great hymns. c1916

INDEX TO STORIES OF HYMNS

Abide with me. (Henry F. Lyte).
Benson. p. 169-178.
Brown. p. 217-219.
Eggleston. p. 8.
Ikenberry. p. 283.
Morrison. p. 191-196
Paine. p. 64-65. 683-684.
Price. p. 98.
Smith N. p. 167-173

Acquaint thyself quickly, O Sinner, with God. (William Knox).
Paine. p. 752-753.

Adeste fideles. (St. Bonaventura?).
Brown. p. 458-460.

Again the circling seasons tell (Hilary of Poitiers).

Again the slowly circling year see Again the circling seasons tell.
Paine. p. 603-605.

Ah, how shall fallen man (Isaac Watts).
Paine. p. 628.

Ah! lovely appearance of death (Charles Wesley).
Paine. p. 479.

Alas, and did my Savior bleed. (Isaac Watts)
Paine. p. 411,438-39.
Price. p. 89.

Alexander. (Mrs. Cecil Frances).
Paine. p. 631.

All glory, laud and honor. (Saint Theodulph, Bishop of Orleans).
Brown. p. 5-8.
Eggleston. p. 2.
Paine. p. 184-185.
Price. p. 39.

All hail the power of Jesus' name. (Edward Perronet).
  Benson 2s. p. 155-166.
  Brown. p. 25-29.
  Eggleston. p. 9-10.
  Ikenberry. p. 284.
  Morrison. p. 152-159.
  Paine. p. 67-69, 166-169, 539, 668-669.
  Price. p. 41.
  Smith N. p. 127-133.
  Smith R. p. 261-283.

All people that on earth do dwell. (William Kethe).
  Benson 2s. p. 1-11.
  Paine. p. 313-314.

All praise to Thee, eternal Lord. (Martin Luther).
  Brown. p. 8-9.
  Paine. p. 14-15.

All praise to Thee my God this night. (Bishop Ken).
  Morrison. p. 80-88.
  Paine. p. 489.

All thanks be to God. (Charles Wesley).
  Paine. p. 232.

All ye that pass by, to Jesus draw nigh. (Charles Wesley).
  Paine. p. 471-472.

"Almost persuaded," now to believe. (Philip P. Bliss).
  Brown. p. 454-455.
  Paine. p. 128-129, 411-412.
  Price. p. 19.
  Smith N. p. 260-261.

Alone, yet not alone am I.
  Paine. p. 522-23.

Along the banks where Babel's current flows. (Psalm 127). (Joel Barlow).
  Paine. p. 589-590.

Always with us, always with us. (Edwin H. Nevin).
  Paine. p. 205.

Am I a soldier of the Cross. (Isaac Watts).
  Paine. p. 24-32, 686-687.

Amazing grace! how sweet the sound. (John Newton).
  Paine. p. 475-476.

America the beautiful. see O beautiful for spacious skies.
Ancient of days. (Bishop Doane).
  Eggleston. p. 12.
And am I only born to die? (Charles Wesley).
  Paine. p. 127-128.
And are we yet alive? (Charles Wesley).
  Paine. p. 751.
And can it be that I should gain? (Charles Wesley).
  Paine. p. 289.
And can we forget in tasting our meat. (Charles Wesley).
  Paine. p. 369.
And canst thou, Sinner, slight. (Mrs. Abrigail B. Hyde).
  Paine. p. 751-752.
And let the feeble body die. (Charles Wesley).
  Paine. p. 266-267.
And must I be to judgment brought. (Charles Wesley).
  Paine. p. 99-100.
And now another day is gone. (Isaac Watts).
  Paine. p. 758-759
And they sang a new song.
  Paine. p. 323-324.
And will the judge descend. (Philip Doddridge).
  Brown. p. 410.
Angels holy, high, and lowly. (John S. Blackie).
  Paine. p. 645-646.
Another year is dawning! (Frances R. Havergal).
  Price. p. 17.
An anthem for Easter. (William Billings).
  Brown. p. 474-476.
Arise, my soul, arise. (Charles Wesley).
  Ikenberry. p. 285.
  Paine. p. 338-339, 526.
  Smith. p. 73.
Arm of the Lord, awake, awake! (Charles Wesley).
  Paine. p. 227-228.
Arne, Thomas Augustine.
  Paine. p. 639-640.

Art thou weary, art thou languid? (St. Stephen the Sabaite). (John M. Neale, tr.).
  Benson 2s. p. 232-244.
  Brown. p. 57.
  Morrison. p. 20-27.
  Paine. p. 574-575, 577-578.
  Price. p. 91.
  Smith N. p. 10-14.
As down in the sunless. (Thomas Moore).
  Brown. p. 243-244.
As I glad bid adieu to the world's fancied pleasure.
  Paine. p. 180.
As thy days, thy strength shall be. (Francis R. Havergal).
  Paine. p. 471.
Asleep in Jesus! blessed sleep. (Mrs. Margaret Mackay).
  Brown. p. 499.
  Paine. p. 379.
At even ere the sun was set. (Henry Twells).
  Paine. p. 586.
Austria. (Tune). (Franz Joseph Haydn).
  Paine. p. 594-595
Ave, Marie Stella. (Venantius Fortunatus, Bishop of Poitiers).
  Brown. p. 356-357.
Ave, sanctissima. (Mrs. Hemans).
  Brown. p. 357-359.
Avon. (Tune). (Hugh Wilson).
  Paine. p. 599-600.
Awake and sing the song. (William Hammond).
  Brown. p. 29-30.
  Paine. p. 215.
Awake, my soul, and with the sun. (Bishop Thomas Ken).
  Paine. p. 753-754.
  Price. p. 108.
Awake my soul, stretch every nerve. (Philip Doddridge).
  Bonsall. p. 16.
  Brown. p. 413-414.
Awake, my soul, to joyful lays. (Samuel Medley).
  Brown. p. 276-277.
Awake, my soul, to meet the day. (Philip Doddridge).
  Paine. p. 197, 494.

Awaked by Sinai's awful sound. (Samuel Occum).
   Brown. p. 267-270.
   Paine. p. 583.
Away in a manger. (Martin Luther).
   Bonsall. p. 34.
Away my unbelieving fear. (Charles Wesley).
   Paine. p. 479-480.
Away with sorrow and fear. (Charles Wesley).
   Paine. p. 80-83.
Bach, John Sebastian.
   Paine. p. 531-532.
Bangor. (Tune).
   Paine. p. 773
The banner of Immanuel! beneath its glorious folds. (Theron Brown).
   Brown. p. 188-189.
Battle hymn of the republic. See—Mine eyes have seen the glory of the coming, etc.
Be not dismayed whate'er betide. (C. D. Martin).
   Price. p. 22.
Be present at our table, Lord! (John Cennick).
   Paine. p. 372-373.
Be Thou exalted, O my God. (Isaac Watts).
   Brown. p. 40, 41-45.
Be Thou, O God, exalted high. (Nahum Tate).
   Brown. p. 11-12.
Beethoven, Ludwig von.
   Paine. p. 251.
Before Jehovah's awful throne. (Isaac Watts).
   Brown. p. 40-41, 41-45.
   Paine. p. 325-326, 339.
   Smith N. 59-60.
Begin my tongue, some heavenly theme. (Isaac Watts).
   Paine. p. 143
Begone unbelief, my Saviour is near. (John Newton).
   Brown. p. 203-204.
Behold a stranger at the door. (Joseph Grigg).
   Paine. p. 255.
Behold the glories of the Lamb. (Isaac Watts).
   Paine. p. 221-222.

Behold the mountain of the Lord. (Michael Bruce).
Paine. p. 38-39.
Behold the Saviour of mankind. (Samuel Wesley).
Paine. p. 12, 365-366.
Price. p. 54.
Beneath Moriah's rocky side. (Robert Murray McCheyne).
Paine. p. 238.
Bernard of Clairvaux.
Paine. p. 543-544.
Berridge, John.
Paine. p. 665-666.
The best fifty American hymns.
Paine. p. 673-675.
Bethany. (Tune). (Lowell Mason).
Paine. p. 606-607.
Beyond the smiling and the weeping. (Horatius Bonar).
Brown. p. 527-528.
Beyond the starry skies. (John Berridge).
Paine. p. 634-635.
The bird let loose in eastern skies. (Thomas Moore).
Brown. p. 244.
The bird with the broken pinion. (Hezekiah Butterworth).
Brown. p. 252-254.
Blessing, honor, thanks and praise. (Charles Wesley).
Paine. p. 666.
Blest be the dear uniting love. (Charles Wesley).
Paine. p. 185-187.
Blest be the tie that binds. (John Fawcett).
Brown. p. 132-133.
Eggleston. p. 13-14.
Ikenberry. p. 286.
Paine. p. 159, 215, 340-342, 510.
Price. p. 21.
Smith N. p. 102-108.
Blest joys from mighty wonders wrought. (Hilary of Poitiers.).
Paine. p. 603-605.
Blest season! which with gladness fraught. (Hilary of Poitiers).
Paine. p. 603-605.

Bliss, Philip.
   Paine. p. 250-251.
   Smith N. p. 258-264.
Blow ye the trumpet, blow!
   Paine. p. 716-717.
Bread of Heaven, on thee we feed. (Josiah Conder).
   Brown. p. 489-490.
Break Thou the bread of life. (Mary A. Lathbury).
   Price. p. 71.
   Bonsall. p. 50.
The breaking waves dashed high. (Mrs. Felicia D. B. Hemans).
   Brown. p. 323-324.
Brethren, while we sojourn here. (Joseph Swain).
   Brown. p. 280-281.
Bright sparkles in the church-yard.
   Paine. p. 452-455.
Brightest and best of the sons of the morning. (Reginald Heber).
   Colson. p. 21-25.
Brightly beams our Father's mercy. (Philip Bliss).
   Paine. p. 71-72.
   Brown. p. 431-432.
   Smith N. p. 261.
   Ikenberry. p. 297.
Bring in the lambs, the tender lambs.
   Paine. p. 379-381.
Build thee more noble mansions. (Oliver W. Holmes).
   Brown. p. 249-250.
By cool Siloam's shady rill. (Reginald Heber).
   Brown. p. 318-319.
By the rude bridge. (Ralph W. Emerson).
   Brown. p. 339-340
Caelbod yn forsee dan yr ian. (Thomas Jones).
   Brown. p. 401.
Cast they bread upon the waters. (Phoebe A. Hanaford).
   Paine. p. 285-286.
A charge to keep I have. (Charles Wesley).
   Brown. p. 274.
The Chariot! the Chariot! its wheels roll in fire. (Henry H. Milman .
   Brown. p. 278-279.
Cheer up, my soul, there is a mercy seat. (John Newton).
   Paine. p. 428-429.

Child of sin and sorrow, filled with dismay. (Thomas Hastings).
   Brown. p. 223.
Child of the regiment. (Charles Jefferys).
   Paine, p. 509-510.
Children of the Heavenly King. (John Cennick).
   Benson 2s. p. 45-55.
Christ for the world we sing. (Samuel Wolcott).
   Bonsall. p. 102.
   Paine. p. 634.
   Price. p. 99.
Christ is born, tell forth His fame. (St. Cosmas).
   Paine. p. 644.
Christ is our corner-stone. (John Chandler, translator).
   Brown. p. 484-485.
Christ, Thou the champion of the band who own. (Matthaus A. von Lowenstern).
   Paine. p. 393.
Christ whose glory fills the skies. (Charles Wesley).
   Paine. p. 233.
Christians, awake, salute the happy morning. (John Byrom).
   Benson 2s. p. 56-67.
   Paine. p. 548.
   Price. p. 69.
Christians, if your hearts are warm. (John Leland).
   Brown. p. 274-276.
The church's one foundation. (Samuel J. Stone).
   Benson 2s. p. 255.
   Bonsall. p. 54.
   Paine. p. 757-758.
Come. (Mrs. James Gibson Johnson).
   Brown. p. 452-454.
Come, all ye chosen saints of God. (Joseph Hart).
   Paine. p. 210-211.
Come gracious Spirit, heavenly dove. (Simon Browne).
   Paine. p. 214.
Come hither, all ye weary souls. (Isaac Watts).
   Brown p. 409-410.
Come, Holy Ghost, in love, shed on us. (Hermannus Contractus) (Ray Palmer tr.).
   Paine. p. 18.
   Smith N. p. 189-191.

Come, Holy Ghost, our souls inspire. See—Creator, Spirit, by whose aid.
Come, Holy Spirit, come! let Thy.... (Joseph Hart).
   Paine. p. 212.
Come, Holy Spirit, Heavenly Dove. (Isaac Watts).
   Brown. p. 282-283.
   Paine. p. 60, 173-175.
Come, Holy Spirit, our souls inspire. See—Creator, Spirit, by whose aid.
Come humble sinner in whose breast. (Edmund Jones).
   Paine. p. 172, 420-422.
Come, let us anew our journey pursue. (Charles Wesley).
   Brown. p. 493-495.
   Paine. p. 185.
Come, let us join our cheerful songs. (Isaac Watts).
   Paine. p. 187-188.
Come let us join our friends above. (Charles Wesley).
   Paine. p. 557-558.
Come let us who in Christ believe. (Charles Wesley).
   Paine. p. 34.
Come, Lord, the drooping sinner cheer.
   Paine. p. 791.
Come, my brethren, let us try.
   Brown. p. 279-280.
Come, my Soul, thou must be waking. (F. R. L. F. Von).
   Paine. p. 774-775.
Come , my soul thy suit prepare. (John Newton).
   Paine. p. 643-644.
Come, O come, Thou quickening Spirit, Thou. (Heinrich Held).
   Paine. p. 602-603.
Come O my soul! in sacred lays. (Thomas Blacklock).
   Paine. p. 685.
Come, Thou Almighty King. (Author unknown).
   Paine. p. 343.
   Price. p. 101.
Come, O Thou all-victorious Lord (Charles Wesley).
   Paine. p. 231-232.
   Price. p. 27.

Come, O Thou traveler unknown. (Charles Wesley).
  Paine. p. 381-382, 559.
Come, oh come! in pious lays. (George Wither).
  Paine. p. 244.
Come, sacred spirit from above. (Philip Doddridge).
  Paine. p. 155-56.
Come saints and sinners hear me tell.
  Paine. p. 440-442.
Come, Saviour, Jesus, from above. (Madame Antoinette Bourignon).
  Paine. p. 209.
Come, Sinner, come. (William E. Witter).
  Brown. p. 417-418.
Come, sinners, to the Gospel feast. (Charles Wesley).
  Paine. p. 35-36.
Come this way, my Father. (A. W. Wildes).
  Paine. p. 660-663.
Come, Thou Fount of every blessing. (Robert Robinson).
  Brown. p. 283-284.
  Ikenberry. p. 287.
  Paine. p. 196, 694-695.
  Price. p. 77.
  Smith N. p. 102-103.
Come, Thou Holy Spirit, come. (Robert II, King of France).
  Brown. p. 57-59.
Come, Thou long-expected Jesus. (Charles Wesley).
  Smith N. p. 73-74.
Come, Thou soul transforming Spirit. (Jonathan Evans).
  Paine. p. 743-744.
Come, Thou Spirit ever living. (Heinrich Held).
  Paine. p. 602-603.
Come to Jesus, come to Jesus.
  Paine. p. 169.
Come to Jesus just now.
  Paine. p. 720-721.
Come unto Me. when shadows darkly gather. (Mrs. Catherine Esling).
  Brown. p. 208-209.
Come unto Me, ye weary. (William C. Dix).
  Price. p. 50.

Come, we who love the Lord. (Isaac Watts).
 Brown. p. 37-40, 41-45.
 Paine. p. 194-195, 223, 273-275, 687-688.
Come, ye disconsolate, where'er ye languish. (Thomas Moore).
 Brown. p. 219-221.
 Paine. p. 62, 311-313.
 Ikenberry. p. 288.
Come ye faithful, raise the strain. (John of Damascus).
 Brown. p. 53-55.
Come ye sinners poor and needy. (Joseph Hart).
 Brown. p. 119-122.
 Paine. p. 211, 443.
The Commandments. Response to be sung after each commandment.
 Bonsall. p. 112.
Commit thou all thy griefs. (Paul Gerhardt).
 Brown. p. 84-88.
 Paine. p. 193-194, 247-248, 393-395, 663-664, 690-691.
Converted tunes.
 Paine. p. 717-720.
Crawford. (Tune).
 Paine. p. 770-771.
Creation. Oratorio. (Francis J. Haydn).
 Paine. p. 555-556, 619.
The Creation. (Tune). (Francis J. Haydn).
 Paine. p. 771.
Creator, Spirit, by whose aid. (Veni Creator). (Rabanus Maurus).
 Paine. p. 249-250.
 Smith N. p. 15-18.
 Morrison. p. 43-51.
Crown Him Lord of all. (Miss L. M. Latimer).
 Paine. p. 706-707.
Crown His head with endless blessing. (William Goode).
 Brown. p. 30-32.
Daily, daily sing the praises. (Sabine Baring-Gould).
 Paine. p. 263-264, 764-765.
Dare to be brave, dare to be true. (W. J. Rooper).
 Bonsall. p. 81.

Daughter of Zion! from the dust. (James Montgomery).
   Brown. p. 486-488.
   Paine. p. 171-172.
Day is dying in the West. (Mary A. Lathbury).
   Eggleston. p. 11.
   Paine. p. 633-634.
The day is past and gone. (John Leland).
   Paine. p. 363-364.
Day of judgment, day of wonders. (John Newton).
   Paine. p. 770.
The day of resurection. (John of Damascus).
   Bonsall. p. 44.
   Brown. p. 53-56.
   Colson. p. 43-46.
   Paine. p. 503-504.
   Price. p. 40.
Day of wrath! that day of burning. (Thomas of Celano).
   Brown. p. 62-65.
   Morrison. p. 28-42.
   Price. p. 92.
   Smith N. p. 19-29.
Dear Christian people, now rejoice. (Martin Luther).
   Paine. p. 179.
Dear Jesus, ever at my side. (Frederick W. Faber).
   Brown. p. 302-303.
Dear Lord and Father of mankind. (John G. Whittier).
   Bonsall. p. 74.
Dear Lord, and master mine. (Thomas H. Gill).
   Paine. p. 688.
Dear Shepherd of Thy people hear. See—O Lord our languid souls inspire.
A deep and holy awe. (Joachim Neander).
   Paine. p. 544-545.
Depth of Mercy! can there be. (Charles Wesley).
   Paine. p. 146, 413, 494-495.
   Price. p. 15.
Did Christ o'er sinners weep. (Benjamin Beddome).
   Brown. p. 160-162.
Dies irae. See—Day of wrath! that day of burning!

Divine and moral songs. (Isaac Watts).
  Paine. p. 223-225.
Dunn, Samuel.
  Paine. p. 614-615.
Dwy aden colomen pe cawn. (Thomas Williams).
  Brown. p. 400-401.
Dykes, John Bacchus.
  Paine. p. 619-621.
Dyma gariad fel y moroedd, Tosturiasthan fel y lli. (William Rees).
  Brown. p. 401-402.
Dyma geidwad i r colledig. (Morgan Rhys).
  Brown. p. 404.
Early, my God, without delay. (Isaac Watts).
  Brown. p. 35-36, 41-45.
The eden of love. (John J. Hicks).
  Brown. p. 272-273.
Elijah—the oratorio. (Felix Mendelssohn-Bartholdy).
  Paine. p. 254-255. 613-614.
Ellerton. (Tune). (E. J. Hopkins).
  Paine. p. 749.
"Emmelar".
  Paine. p. 721.
Equip me for the war. (Charles Wesley).
  Paine. p. 229-230.
Eternal Father, strong to save (William Whiting).
  Brown. p. 369-371.
Eternal light! Eternal light! (Thomas Binney).
  Paine. p. 723.
Eternity. (Mrs. Ellen M. H. Gates).
  Brown. p. 449.
Evan. (Tune). (Lowell Mason).
  Paine. p. 595.
Even me. See—Lord, I hear of showers of blessing.
Eventide. (Tune). William Henry Monk).
  Paine. p. 616-618.
Ewing. (Tune). (Alexander Ewing).
  Paine. p. 605.
The Exile of Erin. See—There came to the beach a poor exile of Erin.

Fairest Lord Jesus! Ruler of all nations. (Munster).
  Bonsall. p. 76.
  Colson. p. 49-54.
  Eggleston. p. 3.
  Paine. p. 755.
Faith of our Fathers, living still. (Frederick W. Faber).
  Bonsall. p. 58.
  Eggleston. p. 11.
  Price. p. 94.
  Smith R. p. 145-168.
Far from the world, O Lord, I flee. (William Cowper).
  Paine. p. 67, 264.
  Smith N. p. 93.
Father by Thy love and power. (Joseph Anstice).
  Paine. p. 205-206.
Father, I own Thy voice. (Samuel Wolcott).
  Paine. p. 644-645.
Father of life and light. (Samuel Fletcher).
  Paine. p. 241-242.
Father of mercies! condescend. (Thomas Morell).
  Paine. p. 242.
Father of mercies, in Thy word. (Anna Steele).
  Benson. p. 191-200.
Father, we thank Thee. (Rebecca J. Weston).
  Bonsall. p. 18-19.
Father, whate'er of earthly bliss. (Anna Steele).
  Brown. p. 196-198.
  Paine. p. 32.
  Smith N. p. 85-88.
Faure, Jean Baptiste.
  Paine. p. 611.
Fawcett, John.
  Paine. p. 611-612.
Fear not, O little flock, the foe. (Gustavus Adolphus).
  Brown. p. 82-84.
  Paine. p. 517-519.
Ein feste Burg (Hymn). See—A mighty fortress is our God.
Ein feste Burg. (Tune). (Martin Luther).
  Paine. p. 686.

Fierce was the wild billow. (Anatolius).
 Brown. p. 354-355.

Finding no place of rest. (John B. Greenwood).
 Paine. p. 568.

Fling out the banner, let it float. (George W. Doane).
 Eggleston. p. 12.
 Price. p. 24.

Flung to the heedless winds. (Martin Luther).
 Paine. p. 374.
 Price. p. 53.

For a season called to part. (John Newton).
 Paine. p. 684-685.

For what shall I praise Thee. (Mrs. Caroline (Fry) Wilson).
 Paine. p. 240.

Forever with the Lord. (James Montgomery).
 Brown. p. 521-523..
 Paine. p. 306.

Forward, be our watchword. (Henry Alford).
 Price. p. 100.

Free from the law, oh, happy condition. (Philip Bliss).
 Paine. p. 138, 745.

Friend after friend departs. (James Montgomery).
 Paine. p. 635.

From all that dwell below the skies. (Isaac Watts).
 Paine. p. 219-221.
 Smith N. p. 58-59.

From dear New England's happy shore.
 Paine. p. 330-332.

From deep distress to Thee I pray. (Martin Luther).
 Paine. p. 432-433.

From every stormy wind that blows. (Hugh Stowell).
 Brown. p. 222-223.
 Paine. p. 170-171.
 Price. p. 31.

From Greenland's icy mountains. (Reginald Heber).
   Benson. p. 63-74.
   Bonsall. p. 98.
   Brown. p. 178-179.
   Ikenberry. p. 289.
   Morrison. p. 236-241.
   Paine. p. 46, 391, 576, 636.
   Price. p. 43.
   Smith N. p. 134-140.
From the cross, uplifted high. (Thomas Haweis).
   Paine. p. 160-161.
From whence does this union arise. (Thomas Baldwin).
   Brown. p. 262-263.
Ganges. (Tune).
   Paine. p. 596.
The gates ajar. (Mrs. Lydia Baxter).
   Smith N. p. 250-251.
The gathering clouds with aspect dark. (John Newton).
   Paine. p. 470-471.
Gauntlet, Henry J.
   Paine. p. 599.
Gentle Jesus, meek and mild. (Charles Wesley).
   Paine. p. 163-165.
   Price. p. 62.
Gently, Lord, oh' gently lead us. (Thomas Hastings).
   Smith N. p. 226-229.
Giardini, Felice de.
   Paine. p. 610-611.
Give me my scallop-shell of quiet. (Sir Walter Raleigh).
   Brown. p. 76-77.
Give me the wings of faith to rise. (Isaac Watts).
   Paine. p. 484.
Give to the winds thy fears. (Paul Gerhardt).
   Paine. p. 247-248, 443-444, 663-664.
Gladly from earth and time I cease. (Martin Luther).
   Paine. p. 601-602.
Gloria Patri. See—Glory be to the Father.
Glorious things of Thee are spoken (John Newton).
   Price. p. 79.

Glory be to the Father (Gloria Patri).
   Price. p. 25.
Glory to God whose sovereign grace. (Charles Wesley).
   Paine. p. 465-466.
Glory to Thee, my God this night. (Bishop Thomas Ken).
   Brown. p. 16-18.
   Paine. p. 63-64, 753-754.
Go and the Savior's love proclaim. (Thomas Morell).
   Paine. p. 242.
Go, on, go on, go on, go on.
   Paine. p. 321.
God be with you till we meet again. (Jeremiah E. Rankin).
   Benson 2s. p. 279-290.
   Brown. p. 496-497.
   Price. p. 109.
God bless our native land. (Charles T. Brooks and John S. Dwight).
   Benson. p. 179-190.
   Brown. p. 347-349.
God calling yet! shall I not hear? (Gerhard Tersteegen).
   Brown . p. 102-105.
   Paine. p. 11.
God is our refuge and our strength.
   Paine. p. 365.
God is the refuge of His saints. (Isaac Watts).
   Paine. p. 45, 272-273, 586-587.
God moves in a mysterious way. (William Cowper).
   Benson 2s. p. 142-153.
   Paine. p. 188-190, 235-236, 387-388.
   Smith N. p. 94.
   Smith R. p. 81-100.
The God of Abraham praise. (Thomas Olivers).
   Brown. p. 18-21.
   Paine. p. 10, 276, 353.
   Price. p. 105.
God of all grace and majesty. (Charles **Wesley**).
   Paine. p. 761-762.
The God of harvest praise. (James Montgomery).
   Brown. p. 480-481.

God of my life, to Thee. (Charles Wesley).
   Paine. p. 262-263.
God of my life, what just return. (Charles Wesley).
   Paine. p. 465.
God of my life, whose gracious power. (Charles Wesley).
   Paine. p. 623-624.
God of our fathers, know of old. (Rudyard Kipling).
   Brown. p. 349-352.
   Price. p. 34.
God of our fathers, whose almighty hand. (Daniel C. Roberts).
   Benson 2s. p. 119-129.
   Eggleston. p. 14-15.
God who madest heaven and earth. (Henry Alberts).
   Paine. p. 245-246.
God's will be done! with joy of heart. (Martin Luther).
   Paine. p. 601-602.
Golden harps are sounding. (Frances Ridley Havergal).
   Paine. p. 571-572.
   Price. p. 46.
Gracious Spirit, dove divine. (John Stocker).
   Paine. p. 291-292.
Gracious Spirit, dwell with me. (Thomas T. Lynch).
   Paine. p. 579.
Grander than ocean's story. (W. F. Sherwin).
   Paine. p. 212.
The great archangel's trump shall sound. (Charles Wesley).
   Paine. p. 496.
Great God of wonders! all Thy ways. (Samuel Davis).
   Paine. p. 482-483.
Great God, the nations of the earth. (William Ward).
   Paine. p. 570.
Great God, we sing that mighty hand. (Philip Doddridge).
   Brown. p. 495-496.
Great God, what do I see and hear? (William B. Collyer).
   Brown. p. 71-74.
   Paine. p. 385-386.
Great God, when I approach Thy throne. (W. H. Bathurst).
   Paine. p. 729.

Greenville. (Tune). (Jean Jacques Rousseau).
　Paine. p. 532-533.
Griffiths, Ann.
　Paine. p. 566.
Guide me, O Thou Great Jehovah. (William Williams).
　Benson 2s. p. 68-79.
　Brown. p. 198-202.
　Morrison. p. 115-121.
　Paine. p. 65-66, 562-563.
　Price. p. 47.
Hail Columbia, Happy Land. (Joseph Hopkinson).
　Brown. p. 331.
　Paine. p. 499-500.
Hail the joyful day's return. (Hilary of Poitiers).
　Paine. p. 603-605.
Hail to the Lord's anointed. (James Montgomery).
　Benson 2s. p. 181-193.
　Brown. p. 175-178.
　Morrison. p. 131-140.
　Paine. p. 3.
　Price. p. 103.
Hail, Tranquil Hour of closing day! (Leonard Bacon).
　Paine. p. 733.
Halle. (Tune).
　Paine. p. 724.
Hallelujah! 'tis done. See—'Tis the promise of God full salvation to give.
Hamburg. (Tune). (Gregory the Great).
　Paine. p. 256-257.
Handel, George Frederick.
　Paine. p. 607-609.
Happy the heart where graces reign. (Isaac Watts).
　Paine. p. 371-372.
Hark from the tombs a doleful sound. (Isaac Watts).
　Paine. p. 727.
Hark, hark, my soul! (Frederick W. Faber).
　Brown. p. 524-525.
Hark, my soul: it is the Lord. (William Cowper).
　Price. p. 80.

Hark the Gospel news is sounding. (Hugh Bourne).
   Paine. p. 627-628.
Hark, the herald angles sing. (Charles Wesley).
   Brown. p. 463.
   Morrison. p. 242-250.
   Paine. p. 489.
   Price. p. 107.
   Smith N. p. 74.
Hark, the voice of Jesus calling. (Daniel March).
   Bonsall. p. 101.
   Paine. p. 632.
   Price. p. 11.
Hark! the voice of love and mercy. (Jonathan Evans).
   Paine. p. 429-431.
Hark! what mean those holy voices. (John Cawood).
   Brown. p. 464-465.
The harmonious blacksmith. (George F. Handel).
   Paine. p. 553.
The harp that once through Tara's halls. (Thomas Moore).
   Brown. p. 328-329.
Harvest home. (Theron Brown).
   Brown. p. 479-480.
Hasten, Lord, the glorious time. (Harriet Auber).
   Brown. p. 168-169.
Hasten sinner, to be wise. (Thomas Scott).
   Brown. p. 410-411.
Hastings. (Tune). (Thomas Hastings).
   Paine. p. 595-596.
Have you on the Lord believed? (Philip Bliss).
   Paine. p. 73-74.
Haydn, Francis Joseph.
   Paine. p. 251-252, 551-552.
He is gone, a cloud of light. (Arthur P. Stanley).
   Paine. p. 549.
He leadeth me! Oh, blessed thought. (Joseph H. Gilmore).
   Bonsall. p. 66.
   Brown. p. 235-236.
   Paine. p. 688-689.
   Price. p. 102.

He will hide me. (Mary E. Servoss).
  Brown. p. 442-445.
Hear, Lord, the song of praise and prayer. (William Cowper).
  Paine. p. 624.
Hear my prayer, O Heavenly Father. (Harriet Parr).
  Paine. p. 237-238.
Hear, O sinner! mercy hails you. (Andrew Reed).
  Paine. p. 431-432.
Hearken to the solemn voice. (Charles Wesley).
  Paine. p. 373-374.
The heavens declare Thy glory Lord. (Isaac Watts).
  Paine. p. 734-735.
Helmsley. (Tune).
  Paine. p. 730.
Herald angels. (Tune). (Mendelssohn).
  Paine. p. 607.
Here behold the tent of meeting. (Ann Griffiiths).
  Brown. p. 396.
Here, O my Lord, I see Thee face to face. (Horatius Bonar).
  Brown. p. 490-491.
Here o'er the earth a stranger I roam.
  Paine. p. 327-328.
Hide Thou me. See—In Thy cleft, O Rock of Ages.
High let us swell our tuneful notes. (Philip Doddridge).
  Paine. p. 246.
High the angel choirs are raising. (Thomas à Kempis).
  Brown. p. 67-68.
His mother's songs.
  Paine p. 702-704.
Ho! my comrades see the signal. (Philip P. Bliss).
  Brown. p. 424.
  Paine. p. 130-131.
  Smith N. p. 261-264.
Hold the fort. See—Ho! my comrades see the signal.
Holy as Thou, O Lord, is none. (Charles Wesley).
  Paine. p. 34-35.
Holy Bible—Book divine. (John Burton).
  Paine. p. 1.

Holy Ghost, dispell our sadness. (Paul Gerhardt).
  Paine. p. 510-511.

Holy Ghost, with light divine. (Andrew Reed).
  Paine. p. 473-474.

Holy, holy, holy, Lord God Almighty. (Reginal Heber).
  Bonsall. p. 78.
  Brown . p. 50-52.
  Colson. p. 57-61.
  Eggleston. p. 11-12.
  Ikenberry. p. 290.
  Morrison. p. 229-235.
  Smith R. p. 169-192.

Holy Night, peaceful night! (Joseph Mohr).
  Bonsall. p. 30.

Holy Spirit! grant us our desire. (Martin Luther).
  Payne. p. 600-602.

Holy Spirit, once again. (Heinrich Held).
  Paine. p. 602-603.

Home sweet home. See—'Mid pleasures and palaces though we may roam.

Hosanna be the children's song. (James Montgomery).
  Paine. p. 762-763.

The hour of my departure's come (Michael Bruce).
  Morrison. p. 167-175.

How are Thy servants blest, O Lord. (Joseph Addison).
  Paine. p. 249.
  Price. p. 14.

How bright appears the morning star. (Philip Nicolai).
  Paine. p. 58-59.

How bright these glorious spirits shine. (W. Cameron).
  Paine. p. 449-451.

How can I sink with such a prop? (Isaac Watts).
  Paine. p. 191-192.

How condescending and how kind. (Isaac Watts).
  Paine. p. 343-344.

How firm a foundation, ye saints of the Lord. (Robert Keene?).
 Benson. *p.* 37-50.
 Bonsall. *p.* 60.
 Brown. *p.* 204-206.
 Eggleston. *p.* 6.
 Ikenberry. *p.* 292-293.
 Paine. *p.* 99, 647.
 Smith N. *p.* 122-126.
How happy every child of grace. (Charles Wesley).
 Paine. *p.* 177, 276-277.
How happy is the child who hears. (Michael Bruce).
 Brown. *p.* 297-298.
How happy is the pilgrim's lot. (John Wesley).
 Brown. *p.* 209-212.
 Paine. *p.* 76-77, 209-210, 366-367.
How many pass the guilty night. (Charles Wesley).
 Paine. *p.* 373-374.
How pleasant 'tis to see. (Isaac Watts).
 Paine. *p.* 333-334.
How sad our state by nature is. (Isaac Watts).
 Paine. *p.* 96-97, 345-346.
How sweet and awful is the place. (Isaac Watts).
 Paine. *p.* 144.
How sweet, how heavenly is the sight. (Joseph Swain).
 Paine. *p.* 5.
How sweet the covenant to remember. (Ann Griffiths).
 Brown. *p.* 396-400.
How sweet the name of Jesus sounds. (John Newton).
 Benson 2s. *p.* 130-141.
 Ikenberry. *p.* 291.
 Paine. *p.* 114, 483-484, 571.
How tedious and tasteless the hours. (John Newton).
 Paine. *p.* 160.
How vain are all things here below. (Isaac Watts).
 Paine. *p.* 259-260.
Hushed was the evening hymn. (James D. Burns).
 Bonsall. *p.* 26.
Hymn to the nativity. (John Milton).
 Brown. *p.* 460-462.

Hymns ancient and modern. (Sir Henry William Baker).
  Paine. p. 617-618.
I am so glad that Our Father in heaven. (Philip Bliss).
  Brown. p. 319-320.
  Paine. p. 133-135, 206, 403-404, 417-418, 549.
I am weary of my sin.
  Paine. p. 310-311.
I ask not now for gold to gild. (John G. Whittier).
  Paine. p. 49.
I cannot always trace the way. (Sir John Bowring).
  Brown. p. 501-502.
I hear the Savior say. (Mrs. Elvina M. Hall).
  Brown. p. 426-427.
  Paine. p. 286, 399-400.
I gave my life for thee. (Frances Ridley Havergal).
  Brown. p. 154-156.
  Paine. p. 135, 573-574, 652.
I have a father in the Promised Land.
  Brown. p. 305.
I have a Savior, He's pleading in glory. (Philip Bliss).
  Paine. p. 131.
I heard the bells (Henry W. Longfellow).
  Bonsall. p. 40.
I heard the voice of Jesus say. (Horatius Bonar).
  Benson 2s. p. 207-219.
  Brown. p. 225-229.
  Morrison. p. 219-228.
  Paine. p. 461-462.
  Smith N. p. 192-197.
I know not the hour when my Lord will come. (Philip Bliss).
  Paine. p. 37.
I know that my Redeemer lives. (Samuel Medley).
  Paine. p. 24.
I know that my Redeemer lives and (Charles Wesley).
  Paine. p. 721-722.
I lay my sins on Jesus. (Horatius Bonar).
  Paine. p. 573, 734.

I love Thy kingdom, Lord. (Timothy Dwight).
   Brown. p. 133-134.
   Paine. p. 213-214.
I love to steal awhile away. (Phebe (H.) Brown).
   Brown. p. 229-233.
   Paine. p. 540-541.
   Price. p. 12.
I love to tell the story. (Katherine Hankey).
   Eggleston. p. 13.
   Paine. p. 534.
   Smith N. p. 244-245.
I need Thee every hour. (Mrs. Annie S. Hawks).
   Brown. p. 153-154.
   Smith N. p. 241-242.
I once was a stranger to grace and to God. (Roebrt M. McCheyne).
   Paine. p. 247.
I remember a voice which once guided my way. See—Come this way my Father.
I saw one hanging on a tree. (John Newton).
   Paine. p. 433.
I think when I read that sweet story of old. (Mrs. Jemima Luke).
   Bonsall. p. 46.
   Brown. p. 305-307.
   Eggleston. p. 12-13.
   Paine. p. 236-237, 268-269.
   Price. p. 84.
I want to be an angel. (Mrs. Sydney P. Gill).
   Paine. p 546.
I was a wandering sheep. (Horatius Bonar).
   Paine. p. 144-145, 734.
   Price. p. 26.
I will sing for Jesus. (Philip Phillips).
   Paine. p. 414.
I will sing you a song of that beautiful land. (Mrs. Ellen M. (H.) Gates).
   Brown. p. 532-534.
I woud be true. (Howard Arnold Walter).
   Eggleston. p. 16.

I would not live alway, I ask not to stay. (William A. Muhlenberg).
   Benson. p. 221-232.
   Brown. p. 157-159.
   Paine. p. 412-413, 582.
I'd be a butterfly. (Thomas H. Bayly).
   Paine. p. 709-710.
If I were a voice, a persuasive voice. (Charles Mackay).
   Brown. p. 182-184.
If you cannot on the ocean. (Mrs. Ellen M. (H.) Gates).
   Brown. p. 256-259.
   Paine. p. 407-409, 637.
   Smith N. p. 239-241.
"Il Trovatore". The anvil chorus. (Verdi).
   Paine. p. 508-509.
I'll praise my Maker, while I've breath. (Isaac Watts).
   Price. p. 70.
I'm a pilgrim, and I'm a stranger. (Mrs. Mary S. (B.) Dana).
   Brown. p. 287-288.
I'm a pilgrim bound for glory.
   Paine. p. 459-460.
I'm a poor sinner and nothing at all.
   Paine. p. 269-270.
I'm but a stranger here. (Thomas R. Taylor).
   Paine. p. 135-137.
   Price. p. 30.
   Brown. p. 300-302.
I'm not ashamed to own my God. (Isaac Watts).
   Brown. p. 107-108.
   Paine. p. 346-348.
Immortal Love, for ever full. (John G. Whittier).
   Smith N. p. 229-231.
In de dark wood. no Indian nigh. (William Apes).
   Brown. p. 263-265.
In Eden—O the memory. (William Williams).
   Brown. p. 383.
In evil long I took delight. (John Newton).
   Paine. p. 322-323.
In grief and fear to Thee, O Lord. (William Bullock).
   Paine. p. 491-492.

In joy and peace I onward fare. (Martin Luther).
   Paine. p. 601-602.
In peace and joy away I go. (Martin Luther).
   Paine. p. 601-602.
In peace and joy I now depart, as. (Martin Luther).
   Paine. p. 601-602.
In peace and joy I now depart, it is. (Martin Luther).
   Paine. p. 601-602.
In sleep's serene oblivion laid. (John Hawkesworth).
   Paine. p. 625.
In some way or other the Lord will provide. (Mrs. Martha A. (W.) Cook).
   Brown. p. 148-150.
In the Christian's home in glory. (Samuel Y. Harmar).
   Paine. p. 122-123, 558-559.
In the cross of Christ, I glory. (Sir John Bowring).
   Brown. p. 97-99.
   Eggeston. p. 7.
   Paine. p. 59, 748-749.
   Price. p. 63.
   Smith N. p. 224-226.
In the hour of trial. (James Montgomery).
   Bonsall. p. 52.
   Paine. p. 624.
In the waves and mighty waters. (David Williams).
   Paine. p. 564-565.
In thine own way, O God of love. (Isaac Watts).
   Paine. p. 270-271.
In Thy cleft, O Rock of Ages. (Fanny Crosby).
   Paine. p. 710-712.
Is this the kind return? (Isaac Watts).
   Brown. p. 108-109.
It came upon the midnight clear. (Edmund H. Sears).
   Bonsall. p. 36.
   Brown. p. 466-468.
It is well with my soul. (Horatio G. Spafford).
   Brown. p. 440-441.
   Smith N. p. 209-213.

It may not be our lot to wield. (John G. Whittier).
Brown. p. 250-252.
Japhet. (Tune).
Paine. p. 749.
Jerusalem divine! when shall I. (Benjamin Rhodes).
Paine. p. 261-262.
Jerusalem my happy home. ("F. B. P.").
Morrison. p. 71-79.
Paine. p. 691-692.
Jerusalem the Glorious. (Bernard of Cluny).
Paine. p. 198-199.
Jerusalem the golden. (Bernard of Cluny).
Brown. p. 509-512.
Morrison. p. 52-60.
Paine. p. 349, 572.
Price. p. 67.
Jesus and shall it ever be. (Joseph Grigg).
Paine. p. 427-428, 495-496.
Jesus at Thy command. (William Williams).
Paine. p. 582.
Jesus, at Thy command I launch into the deep.
Paine. p. 768-769.
Jesus calls us o'er the tumult. (Cecil F. Alexander).
Bonsall. p. 64.
Jesus Christ is risen to-day (Charles Wesley).
Benson. p. 147-154.
Bonsall. p. 42.
Brown. p. 474.
Jesus Christ our true salvation. (John Huss).
Paine. p. 38.
Jesus, I love Thy charming name. (Philip Doddridge).
Brown. p. 117-118.
Paine. p. 51-52, 637.
Jesus, I my cross have taken. (Henry F. Lyte).
Brown. p. 221-222.
Morrison. p. 197-202.
Paine. p. 157, 328-330, 680-681.
Jesus, in Thy dying woes. (Thomas B. Pollock).
Paine. p. 640-641.

Jesus! Jesus! come and save us. (Henry Bateman).
   Paine. p. 587
Jesus keep me near the cross. (Fanny J. Crosby).
   Brown. p. 156-157.
   Paine. p. 178.
Jesus, Lord, Thy servants see. (Benjamin Schmolke).
   Paine. p. 487.
Jesus, lover of my soul. (Charles Wesley).
   Benson 2s. p. 33-44.
   Brown. p. 359-364.
   Ikenberry. p. 294.
   Morrison. p. 107-114.
   Paine. p. 115-121, 228-229, 280-284, 348-349, 573.
   Price. p. 37.
   Smith N. p (.69)-74-83.
   Smith R. p. 17-36.
Jesus loves me. (Anna B. Warner).
   Bonsall. p. 56.
   Paine. p. 278-279, 612-613.
Jesus my all. (Tune).
   Paine. p. 775-776.
Jesus my all to heaven is gone. (John Cennick).
   Brown. p. 126-127.
   Paine. p. 216.
Jesus, my Lord, to Thee I cry. (Eliza H. Hamilton).
   Paine. p. 675-676.
Jesus, my strength, my hope. (Charles Wesley).
   Paine. p. 225-226.
Jesus, Saviour, pilot me. (Edward Hopper).
   Bonsall. p. 96.
   Brown. p. 373-374.
   Eggleston. p. 15.
   Price. p. 76.

Jesus shall reign where'er the sun. (Isaac Watts).
  Brown. p. 165-166.
  Colson. p. 35-39.
  Morrison. p. 122-130.
  Paine. p. 44-45.
  Price. p. 60.
  Smith N. p. 60-62.

Jesus, Shepherd of the Sheep. (Henry Cooke).
  Paine. p. 640.

Jesus show us Thy salvation. (Charles Wesley).
  Paine. p. 476-477.

Jesus, still lead on. (Count Nicholas L. Zinzendorf).
  Paine. p. 57.

Jesus, tender Shepherd, hear me. (Mary L. Duncan).
  Bonsall. p. 24.

Jesus! the name high over all. (Charles Wesley).
  Paine. p. 175-177, 271-272, 286-287, 520-521.

Jesus, the very thought of Thee. (Bernard of Clairvaux).
  Brown. p. 100-102.

Jesus the water of life will give. (Fanny J. Crosby).
  Brown. p. 312-313.

Jesus, these eyes have never seen. (Ray Palmer).
  Paine. p. 515-516.

Jesus, Thou all-redeeming Lord. (Charles Wesley).
  Paine. p. 478.

Jesus, Thou art my righteousness. (Charles Wesley).
  Paine. p. 395-396.

Jesus, Thy blood and righteousness. (Count Nicolaus L. Zinzendorf).
  Brown. p. 91-93.
  Paine. p. 52-53, 209.
  Price. p. 57.

Jesus, where'er Thy people meet. (William Cowper).
  Paine. p. 7-8.
  Price. p. 36.

Jesus, your Lord and King. See—O little children, sing.

Jewels. See—When He cometh, when He cometh.

John Brown's body. (Tune).
  Paine. p. 679-680.

Jordan. (Tune). (William Billings).
  Paine. p. 553-554.
Joy! because the circling year. (Hilary of Poitiers).
  Paine. p. 603-605.
Joy to the world! The Lord is come! (Isaac Watts).
  Brown. p. 166, 463-464.
  Ikenberry. p. 295.
  Paine. p. 87.
Joyful, joyful, we adore Thee. (Henry Van Dyke).
  Eggleston. p. 5-6.
Joyfully, joyfully onward I move. (William Hunter).
  Brown. p. 288-290.
  Paine. p. 699-700.
Just as I am, without one plea. (Charlotte Elliott).
  Benson 2s. p. 194-206.
  Brown. p. 214-216.
  Eggleston. p. 10.
  Ikenberry. p. 296.
  Morrison. p. 160-166.
  Paine, p. 89-95, 208-209, 383-384, 519-520, 546-548, 571, 585, 664-665.
  Price. p. 18.
  Smith N. p. 157-166.
Kathleen Mavourneen.
  Paine. p. 513-514.
Keller's American hymn. (Matthias Keller).
  Brown. p. 343-347.
Kilmarnock. (Tune). (Neil Douglas).
  Paine. p. 616-617.
The King of glory we proclaim. (James Montgomery).
  Paine. p. 569.
The King of love my Shepherd is. (Henry W. Baker).
  Bonsall. p. 90.
  Colson. p. 65-71.
Land ahead! its fruits are waving. (E. Adams).
  Brown. p. 367-369.
  Paine. p. 566-567.
The last hope. (Music by Gottschalk).
  Paine. p. 498-499.

Late, late, so late! and dark the night and chill. (Alfred Tennyson).
   Paine. p. 5-6, 278.
Lead, kindly light, amid the encircling gloom. (John H. Newman).
   Benson. p. 85-96.
   Brown. p. 223-225.
   Morrison. p. 203-211.
   Paine. p. 50.
   Price. p. 61.
   Smith. p. 148-156.
   Smith R. p. 215-238.
Leave God to order all thy ways. (Georg Neumark).
   Paine. p. 218-219, 529-530, 700.
Leominster. (Tune). (George W. Martin).
   Paine. p. 593-594.
Let earth and heaven agree. (Charles Wesley).
   Paine. p. 35.
Let party names no more. (Benjamin Beddome).
   Brown. p. 169.
   Paine. p. 202-203.
Let the lower lights be burning. See—Brightly beams our Father's mercy.
Let us gather up the sunbeams. (Mrs. Albert Smith).
   Paine. p. 650-652.
Let us with a gladsome mind. (John Milton).
   Paine. p. 20.
Life is weary, Savior, take me. (George Neumark).
   Paine. p. 529-530.
A life on the ocean wave. (Epes Sargent).
   Paine. p. 708-709.
Light of the lonely pilgrim's heart. (Edward Denny).
   Paine. p. 756-757.
Listed into the cause of sin. (Charles Wesley).
   Paine. p. 542.
Little travellers Zionward. (James Edmeston).
   Brown. p. 299-300.
Lo! God is here, let us adore. (Gerhard Tersteegen).
   Paine. p. 696-697.
Lo! He comes with clouds descending. (C. Wesley and M. Madan).
   Brown. p. 504-505.
   Paine. p. 489.

Lo, on a narrow neck of land. (Charles Wesley).
    Brown. p. 118-119.
Lo! round the throne, a glorious band. (Rowland Hill).
    Paine. p. 260-261.
Lo! the day of rest declineth. (Chandler Robbins).
    Paine. p. 567-568.
Lo! what a glorious sight appears. (Isaac Watts).
    Brown. p. 505-508.
Lord, a little band and lowly. (Mrs. M. E. Shelly).
    Paine. p. 759.
Lord as a family we meet. (Samuel Fletcher).
    Paine. p. 241-242.
The Lord descended from above. (Thomas Sternhold).
    Brown. p. 15-16.
    Paine. p. 19-20.
Lord dismiss us with thy blessing, bid us now depart in peace. (Robert Hawker).
    Paine. p. 527-528.
Lord dismiss us with Thy blessing, Fill our hearts with joy and peace. (Shirley).
    Paine. p. 531.
Lord, I am Thine, entirely thine. (Samuel Davies).
    Benson 2s. p. 80-92.
    Paine. p. 150-151.
Lord I hear of showers of blessing. (Mrs. Elizabeth Codner).
    Price. p. 74.
    Paine. p. 190, 284, 416.
    Smith N. p. 242-243.
Lord, I know Thy grace is nigh nae. (H. D. Ganse).
    Paine. p. 754.
Lord in the morning thou shall hear. (Isaac Watts).
    Paine. p. 221.
The Lord into His garden comes.
    Brown. p. 277-278.
The Lord is our refuge, the Lord is our Guide. (Henry F. Lyte).
    Paine. p. 512.
Lord, it belongs not to my care. (Richard Baxter).
    Paine. p. 58, 487-488.
Lord Jesus think of me. (Synesius).
    Paine. p. 736.

The Lord my pasture shall prepare. (Joseph Addison).
   Paine. p. 42.
The Lord my shepherd is. (Isaac Watts).
   Paine. p. 54-56.
Lord of all being, throned afar. (Oliver W. Holmes).
   Brown. p. 52.
   Paine. p. 647-648.
   Smith N. p. 231-233.
Lord of Heaven! lone and sad. (Martin Luther).
   Paine. p. 181-183.
Lord of hosts to Thee we raise. (James Montgomery).
   Paine. p. 4.
Lord of the Sabbath, hear our vows. (Philip Doddridge).
   Paine. p. 376.
Lord, speak to me that I may speak. (Frances R. Havergal).
   Eggleston. p. 8.
Lord, teach a little child to pray. (John Ryland).
   Paine. p. 243.
Lord when we bend before Thy throne. (John D. Carlyle).
   Paine. p. 212-213.
Lord, while for all mankind we pray. (John R. Wreford).
   Paine. p. 632-633.
Lord, with glowing heart I'd praise Thee. (Francis S. Key).
   Benson p. 51-61.
   Brown. p. 49-50.
The Lord's my light and saving health.
   Paine. p. 307.
The Lord's my Shepherd. I'll not want. (Francis Rouse).
   Benson 2s. p. 12-21.
   Paine. p. 217-218, 434-436, 678.
The lost chord. (Adelaide A. Proctor).
   Paine. p. 492-493.
Love divine, all love excelling. (Charles Wesley).
   Bonsall. p. 72.
   Brown. p. 111-113.
   Paine. p. 33-34, 739-740.
Magdalena, shout for gladness. (Anon in Latin tr from Latin by C. S. Harrington).
   Brown. p. 472-473.

The Magnificat.
 Brown. p. 10-11.
Maist onie day. (Timothy Swan).
 Paine. p. 712-713.
Majestic sweetness sits enthroned. (Samuel Stennett).
 Brown. p. 23-25.
 Smith R. 123-144.
The Marseillaise hymn. (Roget De Lisle).
 Brown. p. 329-330.
Mason, Lowell.
 Paine. p. 609-610.
Maxim, Granville.
 Paine. p. 550-551.
Maxwelton's braes are bonnie. (William Douglas).
 Paine. p. 149-150.
May God unto us gracious be. (Martin Luther).
 Paine. p. 444-446.
Mear. (Tune).
 Paine. p. 727-729.
Medley, Samuel. 1738.
 Paine. p. 554-555.
Mercy and judgment are my song. (Isaac Watts).
 Paine. p. 676-677.
Merton. (Tune). (Henry K. Oliver).
 Paine. p. 714-715.
The Messiah. (George F. Handel).
 Paine. p. 253-254, 317-319.
Met again in Jesus' name. (John Pyer).
 Paine. p. 513.
Mid pleasures and palaces though we may roam. (John H. Payne).
 Paine. p. 100-102, 307-308, 560-562.
Mid scenes of confusion and creature complaints. (David Denham).
 Brown. p. 134-135.

A mighty fortress is our God. (Martin Luther).
   Benson. p. 155-168.
   Bonsall. p. 92.
   Brown. p. 69-71.
   Eggleston. p. 10-11.
   Morrison. p. 61-70.
   Paine. p. 146-149, 335-336, 583-584.
   Price. p. 85.
   Smith N. p. 30-38.
Mighty God! while angels bless Thee. (Robert Robinson).
   Paine. p. 195-196.
Mine eyes have seen the glory of the coming of the Lord. (Julia Ward Howe).
   Bonsall. p. 108.
   Brown. p. 340-343.
   Eggleston. p. 7-8.
Monson. (Tune).
   Paine. p. 123-125, 580, 680, 700-701.
   Paine. p. 730.
   Price. p. 58-59.
The moonlight sonata. (Ludwig von Beethoven).
   Paine. p. 507-508.
More love to Thee, O Christ. (Mrs. Elizabeth P. Prentiss).
   Smith N. p. 237-239.
The morning light is breaking. (Samuel F. Smith).
   Brown. p. 179-182.
   Paine. p. 656.
   Price. p. 82.
Mt. Blanc. (Tune).
   Paine. p. 255-256.
Mournfully, tenderly, bear on the dead. (Henry S. Washburn).
   Brown. p. 245-247.
Mozart, Johann C. W. A.
   Paine. p. 252-253.
Much in danger oft in woe. See—Oft in danger, oft in woe.
Must Jesus bear the cross alone. (Thomas Shepherd).
   Brown. p. 411-413.
   Paine. p. 183-184.
My ain countree. (Mary Augusta Lee).
   Brown. p. 455-457.

My brother I wish you well.
  Brown. p. 290-292.
My country, 'tis of thee. (Samuel Francis Smith).
  Benson. p. 97-106.
  Bonsall. p. 106.
  Brown. p. 336-339.
  Paine. p. 622-623.
  Price. p. 65.
My days are gliding swiftly by. (David Nelson).
  Paine. p. 199-200.
My faith looks up to Thee. (Ray Palmer).
  Benson. p. 75-84.
  Morrison. p. 212-218.
  Price. p. 7.
  Paine. p. 165-166, 388-391, 516, 564.
  Smith N. p. 183-188.
My God and is Thy table spread. (Philip Doddridge).
  Paine. p. 246.
My God, how endless is the love. (Isaac Watts).
  Brown. p. 105-107.
My God, I love Thee—not because. (St. Francis Xavier).
  Brown. p. 74-76.
  Paine. p. 22-23.
My God, my Father, while I stray. (Charlotte Elliott).
  Paine. p. 572, 745-746.
My gracious Redeemer I love. (Benjamin Francis).
  Brown. p. 132.
My heavenly home is bright and fair. (William Hunter).
  Paine. p. 299-300.
My hope is built on nothing less. (Edward Mote).
  Brown. p. 216-217.
  Paine. p. 244-245.
My Jesus as Thou wilt. (Benjamin Schmolk).
  Brown. p. 499-501.
  Paine. p. 628-629.
My Jesus, I love Thee, I know Thou art mine. (Adoniram J. Gordon).
  Brown. p. 162-164.
My Jesus, stay Thou by me.
  Paine. p. 766-767.

My latest sun is sinking fast. (Jefferson Harcall).
   Paine. p. 279-280.
My Lord and my God! I have trusted in Thee. (Mary Stuart, queen of Scots).
   Brown. p. 77-78.
My Lord, how full of sweet content. (Madam Guyon).
   Brown. p. 190-193.
   Paine. p. 8.
   Price. p. 35.
My soul be on thy guard. (George Heath).
   Brown. p. 143-144.
My soul repeat His praise. (Isaac Watts).
   Paine. p. 74.
My soul through my Redeemer's care. (Charles Wesley).
   Paine. p. 368.
My thoughts on awful subjects roll. (Isaac Watts).
   Paine. p. 267-268.
My times of sorrow and of joy. (Benjamin Beddome).
   Paine. p. 243-244.
Near the cross was Mary weeping. (Jacobus de Benedictus).
   Paine. p. 725.
Nearer, my God, to Thee. (Sarah F. Adams).
   Benson. p. 117-126.
   Bonsall. p. 70.
   Brown. p. 150-153.
   Eggleston. p. 14.
   Ikenberry. p. 298.
   Paine. p. 109-112, 206-207, 300-302, 447-449, 666-668.
   Price. p. 106.
   Smith N. p. 174-182.
   Smith R. p. 101-121.
Nicaea.
   Paine. p. 493-494.
The night was dark; behold, the shade was deeper.
   Paine. p. 397.
No change in time shall ever shock me. (Nahum Tate).
   Brown. p. 193-194.
No more my God, I boast no more. (Isaac Watts).
   Paine. p. 420.

Nobody knows the trouble I see.
 Paine. p. 772-773.
Northfield. (Tune). (Jeremiah Ingalls).
 Paine. p. 535.
Not all the blood of beasts. (Isaac Watts).
 Paine. p. 9, 77, 743.
Not half has ever been told. (John B. Atchison).
 Brown. p. 451-452.
Not now but in the coming years. (Maxwell N. Cornelius).
 Smith N. p. 266-267.
Nothing but leaves, the spirit grieves. (Mrs. Lucy E. Akerman).
 Paine. p. 681-682.
Nothing either great or small. (Rev. Proctor).
 Paine. p. 422-424.
Now begin the heavenly theme. (Martin Madan).
 Paine. p. 577.
Now crave we of the Holy Ghost. (Martin Luther).
 Paine. p. 600-602.
Now hush your cries and shed no tear. (Nicholas Herman).
 Paine. p. 488-489.
Now I have found a friend. (Henry J. M. Hope).
 Paine. p. 349-351.
Now is the accepted time. (John Dobell).
 Paine. p. 61-62.
Now Israel may say and that truly.
 Paine. p. 308.
Now let our souls on wings sublime. (Thomas Gibbons).
 Paine. p. 742-743.
Now on the Holy Ghost we call, for perfect. (Martin Luther).
 Paine. p. 600-602.
Now on the Holy Ghost we call, to give. (Martin Luther).
 Paine. p. 600-602.
Now pray we all God the comforter. (Martin Luther).
 Paine. p. 600-602.
Now pray we to the Holy Ghost. (Martin Luther).
 Paine. p. 600-602.
Now thank we all our God. (Martin Rinkart).
 Paine. p. 15-17.
 Price, p. 45.

Now that the sun is gleaming bright. (John H. Newman).
  Paine. p. 277.
Now the day is over. (S. Baring-Gould).
  Bonsall. p. 28.
Now to the Lord a noble song. (Isaac Watts).
  Brown. p. 33-35.
O beautiful for spacious skies (Katharine Lee Bates).
  Bonsall, p. 110.
  Colson. p. 29-32.
  Eggleston. p. 13.
  Price. p. 23.
O, blessed Savior, in Thy love. (Joseph Stennett).
  Paine. p. 774.
O bliss of the purified! Bliss of the free. (Francis Bottome).
  Brown. p. 433.
O Cana-an, bright Cana-an. (John Maffit).
  Brown. p. 273-274.
O church arise and sing. (Heseziah Butterworth).
  Brown. p. 187-188.
O come and mourn with me awhile. (Frederick W. Faber).
  Paine. p. 511.
O, could I speak the matchless worth. (Samuel Medley).
  Brown. p. 136-137.
O day of rest and gladness. (Christopher Wordsworth).
  Benson, p. 201-210.
  Paine. p. 527.
O do not be discouraged. (John A. Grenade).
  Brown. p. 298-299.
  Paine. p. 170.
O for a closer walk with God. (William Cowper).
  Brown. p. 129-130.
  Ikenberry. p. 299.
  Paine. p. 6-7, 125-126.
  Smith N. p. 93-94.
O for a heart to praise my God. (Charles Wesley).
  Paine. p. 367-368.

O for a thousand tongues to sing. (Charles Wesley).
  Brown. p. 45-48.
  Ikenberry. p. 300.
  Morrison. p. 98-106.
  Paine. p. 233-235.
  Price. p. 68.
  Smith N. p. 72.
O for the death of those. (James Montgomery).
  Paine. p. 2.
O frynan caersalem ceir giveled. (David Charles).
  Brown. p. 403.
O God look down from Heaven we pray. (Martin Luther).
  Paine. p. 337.
O God, my powers are Thine. (Frederick W. Hannan).
  Price. p. 88.
O, God of Abraham ever sure. (Leonard Bacon).
  Paine. p. 740.
O God of Bethel by whose hand. (Philip Doddridge).
  Benson 2s. p. 167-180.
  Paine. p. 514.
  Smith N. p. 65-66.
O God of light and love. (R. C. Watterson).
  Paine. p. 417.
O God, our help in ages past. (Isaac Watts).
  Bonsall. p. 88.
  Smith N. p. 57-58.
O God, why hast Thou cast us off?
  Paine. p. 334-335.
O happy day that fixed my choice. (Philip Doddridge).
  Brown. p. 281-282.
  Ikenberry. p. 301.
  Paine. p. 194.
  Smith N. p. 63-68.
O happy saints that dwell in light. (John Berridge).
  Brown. p. 122-124.
  Paine. p. 378-379.
O help us, Lord; each hour of need. (Henry H. Milman).
  Benson. p. 233-242.

O Holy Father just and true. (John G. Whittier).
  Paine. p. 238-239.
O Holy Ghost, Thou fount of light. (Adam of St. Victor).
  Paine. p. 722-723.
O Jesus Christ, grow Thou in me. (Johann C. Lavater).
  Paine. p. 23-24.
O Jesus, my hope, for me offered up. (Charles Wesley).
  Paine. p. 424-425.
O Jesus, sweet the tears I shed. (Ray Palmer).
  Paine. p. 726.
O Jesus, Thou art standing. (Bishop William W. How).
  Bonsall. p. 68.
  Eggleston. p. 15.
  Price. p. 75.
O joyful sound of Gospel grace. (Charles Wesley).
  Paine. p. 226-227.
O King of Kings, O Lord of hosts. (Henry Burton).
  Price. p. 93.
O little children, sing. (Anna B. Warner).
  Paine. p. 695-696.
O little town of Bethlehem. (Phillips Brooks).
  Benson. p. 1-12.
  Bonsall. p. 38.
  Brown. p. 468-470.
  Colson. p. 15-17.
  Eggleston. p. 6.
  Price. p. 16.
O Lord, I would delight in Thee. (John Ryland).
  Paine. p. 697-698.
O Lord of hosts! Almighty King! (Oliver W. Holmes).
  Paine. p. 425-427.
O Lord our God, with earnest care.
  Paine. p. 581.
O Lord our languid souls inspire. (John Newton).
  Paine. p. 7-8.
O Lord, Thou has rejected us.
  Paine. p. 342-343.
O Lord Thy heavenly grace impart. (John F. Oberlin).
  Paine. p. 545-546.

Index to Stories of Hymns

O Lord Thy work revive. (Mrs. Phoebe H. Brown).
Paine. p. 731.
O Love divine, how sweet thou art! (Charles Wesley).
Paine. p. 466.
O love divine that stooped to share. (Oliver W. Holmes).
Bonsall. p. 48.
Smith N. p. 233.
O love that wilt not let me go. (George Matheson).
Benson 2s. p. 268-278.
Eggleston. p. 9.
Paine. p. 748.
Price. p. 44.
O Love, who formedst me to wear. (Johann Scheffler).
Paine. p. 750.
O Master, it is good to be. (Arthur P. Stanley).
Paine. p. 284-285, 631.
O morning-star, how fair and bright. (Philip Nicolai).
Paine. p. 19.
O Mother dear, Jerusalem. (D. Dickson).
Paine. p. 39-40. 584-585.
O Paradise, O Paradise! Who doth not crave for rest? (Frederick W. Faber)
Brown. p. 525-526.
O perfect Love, all human thought transcending. (Mrs. Dorothy (B.) Gurney).
Brown. p. 503-504.
O Sacred Head, once wounded. (St. Bernard of Clairvaux).
Paine. p. 528, 715-716.
O sancteiddia f'enaid arglewydd. (William Williams).
Brown. p. 405.
O say can you see by the dawn's early light. (Frances Scott Key).
Brown. p. 333-335.
Paine. p. 88-89.
Price. p. 66, 302-303.
O short was His slumber. (Theron Brown).
Brown. p. 476-477.
O sing of Jesus, Lamb of God. (T. C. Kane).
Paine. p. 455.
O sometimes the shadows are deep. (Erastus Johnson).
Paine. p. 43-44.

O still in accents sweet and strong. (Samuel Longfellow).
  Benson. p. 137-146.
O tell me no more of this world's vain store. (John Gambold).
  Paine. p. 460-461.
O that the Lord would gracious be. (Martin Luther).
  Paine. p. 498.
O think of the home over there. (De Witt W. Huntington).
  Brown. p. 436-437.
O Thou, from whom all goodnes flows. (Thomas Haweis).
  Paine. p. 52, 358-359, 648-649.
O Thou God, who hearest prayer. (Josiah Conder).
  Paine. p. 689
O thou my soul, bless God the Lord. (Psalm 103. Scotch).
  Paine. p. 386-387.
O Thou my soul forget no more. (Krishnu Pal).
  Brown. p. 491-492.
  Paine. p. 731-732.
O Thou to whom in ancient time. (John Pierpont).
  Paine. p. 241.
O Thou who camest from above. (Charles Wesley).
  Paine. p. 533.
O Thou who dry'st the mourner's tears. (Thomas Moore).
  Brown. p. 244.
O where are kings and empires now? (Cleveland Coxe).
  Paine. p. 352.
O where are the reapers? (Eben E. Rexford).
  Brown. p. 439-440.
O where shall rest be found. (James Montgomery).
  Paine. p. 190-191, 290.
O worship the King all glorious above. (Sir Robert Grant).
  Brown. p. 21-23.
O Zion, afflicted with wave upon wave. (James Grant).
  Paine. p. 246-247.
The ocean hath no danger. (Godfrey Thring).
  Brown. p. 371-372.
Ode on science. (Janaziah (or Jazariah) Summer).
  Brown. p. 330-331.
O'er the gloomy hills of darkness. (William Williams).
  Brown. p. 166-168.
  Paine. p. 606.

O'er those gloomy hills of darkness. (William Williams).
   Paine. p. 172-173, 592-593.
Of all that decks the field or bower. (Abdul Messeeh).
   Paine. p. 74-76.
Oft in danger, oft in woe. (Henry K. White).
   Paine. p. 490.
   Price. p. 64.
Oft in sorrow, oft in woe. See—Oft in danger, oft in woe.
Oh, Christ, He is the fountain. (Mrs. Anne R. Cousin).
   Paine. p. 737-738.
Oh, come and let us all with one accord. (Anon.).
   Paine. p. 694.
Oh, Galilee, sweet Galilee. (Robert Morris).
   Brown. p. 260-261.
Oh give ye praise unto the Lord.
   Paine. p. 309-310.
Oh! Holy Ghost to Thee we pray. (Martin Luther).
   Paine. p. 600-602.
Oh Lord of hosts whose glory fills the bounds of the eternal hills. (J. M. Neale)
   Brown. p. 485-486.
Oh! mean may seem this house of clay. (Thomas H. Gill).
   Paine. p. 590.
Oh say! can you see by the dawn's early light. See—O say can you see etc.
Oh! sing to me of heaven. (Mrs. Mary S. B. Shindler).
   Paine. p. 69-71.
Oh, sweetly breathe the lyres above. (Ray Palmer).
   Paine. p. 693.
Oh, why should the spirit of mortal be proud? (William Knox).
   Brown. p. 238-240.
   Paine. p. 87.
Old Chester. (William Billings).
   Brown. p. 331-333.
Old Hundred. (Tune).
   Paine. p. 621-622.
The old oaken bucket. (Samuel Woodworth).
   Paine. p. 682.
The old Psalm tune. (Mrs. Harriet Beecher Stove).
   Paine p. 704-706.

Olmutz. (Tune). (Gregory the Great).
  Paine. p. 256-257.
On Jordan's stormy banks I stand. (Samuel Stennett).
  Paine. p. 382, 759-761.
On the fount of life eternal. (Peter Damiani).
  Paine. p. 778-779.
On the mountain top appearing. (Thomas Kelly).
  Brown. p. 173-174.
  Paine. p. 7, 763-764.
On this stone, now laid with prayer. (John Pierpont).
  Paine. p. 375.
Once in Royal David's City. (Cecil F. Alexander).
  Bonsall. p. 32.
One more day's work for Jesus. (Anna Warner).
  Brown. p. 418-419.
One sweetly solemn thought. (Phoebe Cary).
  Brown. p. 529-532.
  Ikenberry. p. 302.
  Paine. p. 126-127, 404-407.
  Smith N. p. 203-208.
Only an armor-bearer. (Philip P. Bliss).
  Smith N. p. 261.
Only remembered. (Horatius Bonar).
  Brown. p. 308-310.
Only waiting till the shadows. (Frances Laughton).
  Paine. p. 325.
Onward, Christian soldiers. (Sabine Baring-Gould).
  Benson. p. 107-116. ....
  Bonsall. p. 82.
  Brown. p. 185-186.
  Eggleston. p. 12.
  Paine. p. 530-531
  Price. p. 55.
  Smith R. p. 239-259.
Onward ride in triumph, Jesus. (William Williams).
  Brown. p. 382-383.
Our fathers' God! from out whose hand. (John G. Whittier).
  Smith N. p. 231.
Our God, our help in ages past. See—O God, our help in ages past.

Our Father, God, who art in Heaven. (Adoniram Judson).
  Paine. p. 239-240.
Our thought of Thee is glad with hope. (John G. Whittier).
  Price. p. 32.
Out on an ocean all boundles we ride. (William F. Warson).
  Paine. p. 398-399.
Palestrina, Giovanni Pierluigi da.
  Paine. p. 580-581.
Palm branches. (Jean B. Faure).
  Brown. p. 470-471.
Pass me not, O gentile Savior by. (Fanny J. Crosby).
  Paine. p. 402-403.
  Smith N. p. 234-236. ....
Pax tecum. (Tune). (G. T. Caldbeck).
  Paine. p. 596.
Peace, doubting heart! my God's I am. (Charles Wesley).
  Paine. p. 497, 756.
Peace my heart, be calm, be still. (Charles Wesley).
  Paine. p. 536.
Peace, perfect peace. (Bishop Edward H. Bickersteth).
  Price. p. 8.
Peace, troubled soul, thou need'st not fear. (Samuel Ecking).
  Paine. p. 316-317.
Peace, troubled soul, whose plantive moan. (Sir Walter Shirley).
  Brown. p. 202-203.
People of the living God. (James Montgomery).
  Brown. p. 144-146.
  Paine. p. 290.
Pilgrim burdened with thy sin. (George Crabbe).
  Paine. p. 324-325.
A pilgrim through this lonely world. (Sir Edward Denny).
  Paine. p. 752.
Plunged in a gulf of dark despair. (Isaac Watts).
  Paine. p. 485.
A poor wayfaring man of grief. (James Montgomery).
  Brown. p. 285.
Portuguese hymn. (Tune).
  Paine. p. 693-694.

Praise God from whom all blessings flow. (Bishop Thomas Ken).
   Bonsall. p. 114.
   Brown. p. 13-14.
   Eggleston. p. 3-4.
   Paine. p. 161-163, 332-333, 653.
   Price. p. 86.
   Smith N. p. 39-48.
Praise the Lord, His glories show. (Henry F. Lyte).
   Paine. p. 377.
Praise to the Holiest in the height. (John H. Newman).
   Paine. p. 758.
   Price. p. 13.
Praise ye the Lord! 'Tis good to raise. (Isaac Watts).
   Paine. p. 371.
Prayer is the soul's sincere desire. (James Montgomery).
   Paine. p. 4, 653-654.
   Smith N. p. 220-224.
The praying spirit breathe. (Charles Wesley).
   Paine. p. 478-479.
Precious promise God hath given. (Nathaniel Niles).
   Paine. p. 754.
The prodigal child. (Mrs. Ellen M. H. Gates).
   Brown. p. 430.
Pull for the shore. (Philip P. Bliss).
   Brown. p. 372-373.
   Smith N. p. 261.
Rain on the roof. (Coates Kinney)
   Paine. p. 707-708.
Rejoice and be glad. (Horatius Bonar).
   Brown. p. 415-417.
Rescue the perishing, care for the dying. (Fanny J. Crosby).
   Bonsall. p. 86.
   Brown. p. 425.
   Paine. p. 702.
   Smith N. p. 237.
Return, O wanderer to thy home. (Thomas Hastings).
   Paine. p. 636.
Revive Thy work, O Lord. (Albert Midlane).
   Brown. p. 445-446.

Rhyfeddodan dydd yr adgyfodidd.
> Brown. p. 402-403.

Righteous God whose vengeful vials. (Charles Wesley).
> Paine. p. 468.

Rise, crowned with light. (Alexander Pope).
> Brown. p. 238.
> Paine. p. 13.

Rise, my soul, and stretch thy wings. (Robert Seagrave).
> Brown. p. 94-97.

Rock of ages cleft for me. (Augustus M. Toplady).
> Benson 2s. p. 104-118.
> Brown. p. 137-143.
> Ikenberry. p. 303.
> Morrison. p. 89-97.
> Paine. p. 47-49, 102-108, 353-358, 489, 654-655.
> Price. p. 97.
> Smith N. p. 121.
> Smith R. p. 193-214.

Rossini, Gioachino Antonio.
> Paine. p. 777.

Round roll the weeks our hearts to greet. (Hilary of Poitiers).
> Paine. p. 603-605.

The royal banners forward go. (Venantius Fortunatus).
> Paine. p. 21-22.

Safe in the arms of Jesus. (Fanny J. Crossby).
> Brown. p. 540-541.
> Paine. p. 178-179, 304-305, 360-363, 692-693.
> Smith N. p. 237.

Sailor, though the darkness gathers. (Philip Bliss).
> Paine. p. 72.

St. Alphege. (Tune). (Henry J. Gauntlett).
> Paine. p. 619.

St. Anne. (Tune).
> Paine. p. 744.

St. Matthew. (Tune).(William Croft).
> Paine. p. 617.

Salvation! O the joyful sound! (Isaac Watts).
> Paine. p. 369-370.

The sands of time are sinking. (Mrs. Anne R. Cousin).
  Brown. p. 78-82.
  Paine. p. 737-738.
  Price. p. 90.
Saviour, again to Thy dear name we raise. (John Ellerton).
  Benson 2s. p. 245-254.
Saviour, breathe an evening blessing. (James Edmeston).
  Paine. p. 213.
  Price. p. 28.
Saviour, like a Shepherd lead us. (Mrs. Dorothy A. Thrupp).
  Brown. p. 310-311.
Saviour, Thy dying love. (Sylvester D. Phelps).
  Brown. p. 147-148.
Savour visit Thy plantation. (John Newton).
  Paine. p. 629-631. ....
Say, Brothers, will you meet us.
  Paine. p. 409-410.
Scatter seeds of sunshine. (Mary L. Riley).
  Brown. p. 317-318.
Schubert, Franz Peter.
  Paine. p. 776-777.
See how great a flame. (Charles Wesley).
  Paine. p. 226.
Selma. (Tune). (Robert A. Smith).
  Paine p. 597-598.
Servant of God, well done! (James Montgomery).
  Paine. p. 757.
  Price. p. 33
Shall we gather at the river. (Robert Lowry).
  Paine. p. 141-143, 757.
  Smith N. p. 264-266.
Shepherd of tender youth. (Clement of Alexandria).
  Benson. p. 243-252.
  Brown. p. 293-296.
  Paine. p. 21.
  Price. p. 52.
Shine, Mighty God, on Zion shine. (Isaac Watts).
  Paine. p. 741-742.

Shirland. (Tune). (Samuel Stanley).
   Paine. p. 597.
Show pity, Lord, O Lord, forgive. (Isaac Watts).
   Paine. p. 9, 151-155.
Shrinking from the cold hand of death. (Charles Wesley).
   Brown. p. 520- 521.
   Paine. p. 410.
Since all the varying scenes of time. (James Hervey).
   Paine. p. 32-33.
Since Jesus truly did appear. (John Berridge).
   Brown. p. 503.
Singing for Jesus, singing for Jesus. (Fanny J. Crosby).
   Paine. p. 150.
So fades the lovely blooming flower. (Anna Steele,).
   Paine. p. 200-202.
Softly and tenderly Jesus is calling.
   Paine. p. 671-673.
Softly now the light of day. (Bishop Doane).
   Brown. p. 482-484.
Some day the silver cord will break. (Fanny J. Crosby).
   Smith R. p. 57-80.
Sometime we'll understand. See—Not now but in the coming years.
Sometimes a light surprises. (William Cowper).
   Paine. p. 750.
The Son of God goes forth to war. (Reginald Heber).
   Bonsall. p. 104.
The Son of God! the Lord of life. (George Mogridge).
   Paine. p. 523-524.
The song of the shirt. (Thomas Hood).
   Paine. p. 683.
Sound the loud timbrel. (Thomas Moore).
   Brown. p. 326-328.
Sovereign ruler of the skies. (John Ryland).
   Paine. p. 351.
Sow in the morn thy seed. (James Montgomery).
   Paine. p. 755.
   Price. p. 78.

Sowing the seed by the daylight fair. (Mrs. Emily S. Oakey).
    Brown. p. 434-436.
    Paine. p. 139-140, 305.
    Smith N. p. 245-247.
The spacious firmament on high. (Joseph Addison).
    Paine. p. 42.
    Price. p. 96.
Speak gently, it is better far. (David Bates).
    Paine. p. 505-507.
Speed away! speed away on your mission of light. (Fanny J. Crosby).
    Brown. p. 184-185.
Spirit leave thy house of clay. (James Montgomery).
    Paine. p. 511-512.
Stabat mater. (Music). G. A. Rossini).
    Paine. p. 769.
Stand! the ground's your own, my braves. (John Pierpont).
    Brown. p. 335-336.
Stand up, and bless the Lord. (James Montgomery).
    Paine. p. 2.
Stand up, stand up for Jesus. (George Duffield, Jr.).
    Benson. p. 13-24.
    Bonsall. p. 84.
    Eggleston. p. 10.
    Paine. p. 155, 591.
    Price. p. 42.
    Smith N. p. 198-202.
    Smith R. p. 37-55.
The Star spangled banner. See—O say can you see by the dawn's early light.
Stay, thou insulted spirit, stay. (Charles Wesley).
    Paine. p. 477.
Steele, Anne.
    Paine. p. 542-543.
Still, still with Thee. (Mrs. Harriet Beecher Stowe).
    Brown. p. 481-482.
Strong Son of God, Immortal Son. (Alfred Tennyson).
    Paine. p. 625.
    Price. p. 73.
Sullivan, Sir Arthur S.
    Paine. p. 733.

Sun of my soul, Thou Saviour dear. (John Keble).
   Benson. p. 25-36.
   Brown. p. 159-160.
   Morrison. p. 184-190.
   Price. p. 81.
   Smith N. p. 141-147.

Sunset and evening star. (Alfred Tennyson).
   Benson. p. 263-272.
   Brown. p. 538-539.

Sweet hour of prayer, sweet hour of prayer. (William W. Walford).
   Brown. p. 432-433.
   Paine. p. 447-449.

Sweet is the day of sacred rest. (Isaac Watts).
   Brown. p. 488-489.

Sweet is the work, My God, my King. (Isaac Watts).
   Brown. p. 37, 41-45.
   Paine. p. 158.

Sweet the moments, rich in blessing. (Sir Walter Shirley and James O. Allen).
   Benson 2s. p. 93-103.
   Brown. p. 127-129.
   Price. p. 10.

Sweet the time, exceeding sweet. (George Burder).
   Paine. p. 23.

Sweet was the time when first I felt. (John Newton).
   Paine. p. 121-122.

Take me, O my Father, take me. (Ray Palmer).
   Paine. p. 655.

Take my life, and let it be. (Frances R. Havergal).
   Benson. p. 211-220.
   Paine. p. 626, 737.
   Price. p. 83.
   Smith N. p. 214-219.

Take the name of Jesus with you. (Lydia Baxter).
   Paine. p. 414-416.

Tallis' evening hymn.
   Brown. p. 16-18.

Te Deum laudamus. (Ambrose, Bishop of Milan).
  Brown. p. 1-5.
  Morrison. p. 9-19.
  Paine. p. 257-258.
  Smith N. p. 1-9.
Teach me my God and King. (George Herbert).
  Paine. p. 17-18.
Tell it out among the nations. (Frances R. Havergal).
  Paine. p. 570.
Tell me not in mournful numbers. (Henry W. Longfellow).
  Brown. p. 248-249.
Tell me the old, old story. (Katherine Hankey).
  Brown. p. 427-430.
  Paine. p. 534.
  Price. p. 56.
  Smith N. p. 243-244.
That day of wrath, that dreadful day. (Sir Walter Scott).
  Paine. p. 524-526.
There are lonely hearts to cherish. (George Cooper).
  Brown. p. 312.
There came to the beach a poor exile of Erin. (Thomas Campbell).
  Paine. p. 588-589.
There is a book that all may read. (John Keble).
  Paine. p. 66.
There is a city great and strong. (Dennis Wortman).
  Paine. p. 735-736.
There is a fountain filled with blood. (William Cowper).
  Morrison. p. 141-151.
  Paine. p. 84-86, 293-299, 522.
  Smith N. p. 94-101.
There is a gate that stands ajar. (Lydia Baxter).
  Paine. p. 451-452.
There is a God that reigns above. (Isaac Watts).
  Paine. p. 320.
There is a green hill far away. (Cecil Frances Humphreys).
  Benson 2s. p. 220-231.
  Brown. p. 414-415.

There is a happy land. (Andrew Young).
  Brown. p. 304.
  Paine. p. 314-316, 659-660, 747-748.
There is a land immortal. (Thomas MacKeller).
  Paine. p. 656-657.
There is a land of pure delight (Isaac Watts).
  Benson 2s. p. 22-32.
  Paine. p. 40, 642-643.
  Price. p. 72.
There is a spot to me more dear. (William Hunter).
  Paine. p. 669-671.
There is an eye that never sleeps. (J. C. Wallace).
  Paine. p. 649-650.
There is no flock however watched and tended. (Henry W. Longfellow.).
  Paine. p. 36-37.
There were ninety and nine that safely lay. (Mrs. Elizabeth C. Clephane).
  Brown. p. 422-424.
  Paine. p. 60-61.
  Smith N. p. 251-256.
There's a friend for little children.. (Albert Midlane).
  Price. p. 29.
There's a land that is fairer than day. (Sanford F. Bennett).
  Brown. p. 534-538.
There's a light in the window for thee, Brother. (Philip P. Bliss).
  Paine. p. 73.
There's a wideness in God's mercy. (Frederick W. Faber).
  Brown. p. 233-235.
They that toil upon the deep. (James Montgomery).
  Brown. p. 353-354.
Thine earthy Sabbaths, Lord, we love. (Philip Doddridge).
  Paine. p. 197-198.
Thine forever! God of love. (Mary F. Maude).
  Benson. p. 253-262.
This is my Father's world. (Maltbie D. Babcock).
  Colson. p. 75-81.
Thou art gone to the grave but we will not deplore thee. (Reginald Heber).
  Paine. p. 657.
Thou art, O God, the life and light. (Thomas Moore).
  Brown. p. 244-245.

Thou dear Redeemer, dying Lamb. (John Cennick).
   Brown. p. 124-125.
Thou God of truth and love. (Charles Wesley).
   Paine. p. 462-463.
Thou hidden love of God whose height. (Gerhard Tersteegen).
   Paine. p. 496-497.
Thou Holy Spirit, we pray to Thee. (Martin Luther).
   Paine. p. 600-602.
Thou soft flowing Kedron, by thy silver stream. (Madam De Fleury).
   Paine. p. 491.
Thou Son of God, whose flaming eyes. (Charles Wesley).
   Paine. p. 97-98.
Thou, too, sail on, O Ship of state. (Henry W. Longfellow).
   Brown. p. 349.
Though now the nations sit beneath.
   Paine. p. 738-739.
Though troubles assail, and dangers affright. (John Newton).
   Paine. p. 203-204.
Three fishes went sailing out into the West. (Charles Kingsley).
   Paine. p. 560.
Through the night of doubt and sorrow. (Bernhardt S. Ingemann).
   Price. p. 95.
Through the valley of the shadow I must go. (Philip P. Bliss).
   Paine. p. 138-139.
Throw out the Life-line. (Edward S. Ufford).
   Brown. p. 374-377.
Thy life was given for me. (Frances R. Havergal).
   Price. p. 48-49.
Thy will be done! with joyful heart. (Martin Luther).
   Paine. p. 601-602.
Thy word, O Lord, Thy precious word alone. (Alfred Midlane).
   Paine. p. 626.
Time is winging us away. (John Burton).
   Paine. p. 218.
'Tis religion that can give. (Mary Masters).
   Brown. p. 303.
   Paine. p. 556-557.
'Tis the old ship of Zion, Hallelujah!
   Brown. p. 290.

'Tis the promise of God full salvation to give. (Philip P. Bliss).
   Brown. p. 422.
   Paine. p. 131-132.
To Heaven I lift my waiting eyes. (Isaac Watts).
   Paine. p. 468-469.
To leave my dear friends and from neighbors to part. (John Osborne).
   Brown. p. 146-147.
To the work, to the work. (Fanny J. Crossby).
   Brown. p. 438-439.
To Thee I lift my soul.
   Paine. p. 320-321.
To Thee Thou Holy Spirit now. (Martin Luther).
   Paine. p. 600-602.
To Thy temple we repair. (James Montgomery).
   Paine. p. 202.
To us salvation now has come. (Paul Speratus).
   Paine. p. 336.
Today the Savior calls. (Samuel F. Smith).
   Paine. p. 401-402, 633.
To-day thou livest yet.
   Paine. p. 765-766.
Too late! too late! ye cannot enter new. (Alfred Tennyson).
   Brown. p. 259-260.
Triumph by and by. (Christopher R. Blackall).
   Brown. p. 449-450.
Triumphant Zion, lift thy head. (Philip Doddridge).
   Brown. p. 519-520.
True love can ne'er forget. (Samuel Lover).
   Paine. p. 500-501.
The turf shall be my fragrant shrine. (Thomas Moore).
   Brown. p. 244.
'Twas on that night, when doom'd to know. (John Morrison).
   Morrison. p. 176-183.
Ultima Thule. (Seneca).
   Brown. p. 321-322.
Under the palms. (George F. Root and Hezekiah Butterworth).
   Brown. p. 254-255.
Upward I lift mine eyes. (Isaac Watts).
   Paine. p. 657-658.

Vain, delusive world adieu. (Charles Wesley).
  Paine. p. 192-193, 514-515.
Veni Creator Spiritus. See—Creator, Spirit, by whose aid.
Veni sancte Spiritus. See—Come, Holy Ghost, in love.
Vital spark of heavenly flame. (Alexander Pope).
  Brown. p. 515-517.
  Paine. p. 14.
The voice of free grace cries, "Escape to the mountain." (Richard Burdsall).
  Paine. p. 439-440, 758.
Waiting and watching for me. (Mrs. Marianne F. Hearn).
  Brown. p. 441-442.
Wake, awake, for night is flying. (Philip Nicolai).
  Paine. p. 19.
Walk in the light! so shalt thou know. (Bernard Barton).
  Paine. p. 51.
Walther, Johann.
  Paine. p. 637-639.
Watchman, tell us of the night. (Sir John Bowring).
  Brown. p. 170-171.
  Colson. p. 9-11.
  Eggleston. p. 15.
  Paine. p. 559-560.
  Smith N. p. 226.
We are joyously voyaging over the main. (William Hunter).
  Paine. p. 436-438.
We come to the fountain we stand by the wave. (George W. Bethune).
  Paine. p. 658.
We plow the fields, and scatter. (Matthias Claudius).
  Brown. p. 478.
  Colson. p. 3-5.
  Price. p. 104.
We sat down and wept by the waters. (Lord Byron).
  Brown. p. 241-243.
We shall meet beyond the river. (John Atkinson).
  Brown. p. 528-529.
  Paine. p. 690.
We speak of the realms of the blest. (Mrs. Elizabeth Mills).
  Brown. p. 307-308.
  Paine. p. 239.

Webb. (Tune). (George J. Webb).
  Paine. p. 615.
Welcome, happy morning, age to age shall say .(Venantius Honorius Clementianus Fortunatus).
  Paine. p. 440, 726-727.
  Price. p. 51.
Wellesley. (Tune). Lizzie S. Tourgee).
  Paine. p. 535.
We're traveling home to heaven above. (Charles Wesley).
  Paine. p. 108-109, 273.
Wesley's hymns for children.
  Paine. p. 287-289.
Westward the course of empire. (George Berkeley).
  Brown. p. 324-326.
What a friend we have in Jesus. (Joseph Scriven).
  Bansall. p. 94.
  Brown. p. 425-426.
  Paine. p. 216-217, 418-420.
  Price. p. 87.
What can wash away my stain? (Robert Lowry).
  Paine. p. 627.
What means this eager, anxious throng? (Etta Campbell).
  Paine. p. 303-304, 521.
  Smith N. p. 247-249.
What our Father does is well. (Benjamin Schmolke).
  Paine. p. 50.
What shall the harvest be. See—Sowing the seed by the daylight fair.
What various hindrances we meet. (William Cowper).
  Brown. p. 131.
When Abraham's servant to procure. (John Ryland).
  Paine. p. 243.
When all Thy mercies, O my God. (Joseph Addison).
  Brown. p. 113-116.
  Paine. p. 41-42.
When doomed to death, the apostle lay. (William C. Bryant).
  Paine. p. 375.
When for eternal worlds I steer. (Jabez Swain).
  Brown. p. 286-287.

When gathering clouds around I view. (Sir Robet Grant).
    Brown. p. 212-213.
When He cometh, when He cometh. (William O. Cushing).
    Brown. p. 314-317.
    Paine. p. 304.
    Smith N. p. 266.
When He cometh, when He cometh. (Tune). (George F. Root).
    Paine. p. 216-217.
When I can read my title clear. (Isaac Watts).
    Brown. p. 514-515.
    Paine. p. 112-114.
When I survey the wondrous cross. (Isaac Watts).
    Benson. p. 127-136.
    Brown. p. 109-111.
    Paine. p. 173, 748-749.
    Price. p. 38.
    Smith N. p. 49-57.
When Israel freed from Pharoah's hand. (Isaac Watts).
    Paine. p. 292.
When Israel of the Lord beloved. (Sir Walter Scott).
    Brown. p. 240-241.
    Paine. p. 469-470.
When Jesus comes. (Philip P. Bliss).
    Brown. p. 437-438.
When Jordan hushed his water still. (Thomas Campbell).
    Paine. p. 3.
When marshalled on the nightly plain. (Henry K. White).
    Brown. p. 364-367.
    Paine. p. 204-205, 265-266.
When morning, gilds the sky. (German, 19th Century. Tr. by Edward Caswell).
    Bonsall. p. 20.
When my final farewell to the world I have said. (M. F. Hearn).
    Paine. p. 641-642.
When shall my wondering soul begin? (Charles Wesley).
    Paine. p. 789.
When shall we all meet again?
    Brown. p. 265-267.
When the harvest is past and the summer is gone. (Samuel F. Smith).
    Paine. p. 392-393.

When Thou, my righteous Judge, shalt come. (Lady Selina Huntington).
  Brown. p. 88-91.
  Paine. p. 537.
Where cross the crowded ways of life. (Frank M. North).
  Price. p. 9.
Where is my wandering boy to-night. (Robert Lowry).
  Brown. p. 446-448.
Where now are the Hebrew children.
  Brown. p. 270-272.
While on the verge of life I stand. (Philip Doddridge).
  Paine. p. 95-96.
While shepherds watched their flocks. (Nahum Tate).
  Brown. p. 465-466.
While Thee I seek, Protecting power. (Helen M. Williams).
  Brown. p. 125-126, 207-208.
While with ceaseless course the sun. (John Newton).
  Brown. p. 493-495.
Who is on the Lord's side? (Frances R. Havergal).
  Bonsall. p. 62.
The whole world was lost in the darkness of sin. (Philip P. Bliss).
  Price. p. 20.
Whosoever heareth, shout, shout the sound. (Philip P. Bliss).
  Paine. p. 540.
Whosoever will. (Philip P. Bliss).
  Smith N. p. 260.
Why do we mourn departed friends. (Isaac Watts).
  Brown. p. 194-196.
Why should the children of a King? (Isaac Watts).
  Paine. p. 222.
Why should we start and fear to die? (Isaac Watts).
  Brown. p. 512-514.
Why those fears? behold, 'tis Jesus. (Thomas Kelly).
  Paine. p. 504-505.
With peace and joy from earth I go. (Martin Luther).
  Paine. p. 601-602.
With songs and honors sounding loud. (Isaac Watts).
  Brown. p. 479.
With tearful eyes I look around. (Charlotte Elliott).
  Paine. p. 207-208.

Woodman spare that tree. (George P. Morris).
  Paine. p. 698-699.
Work for the night is coming. (Anna L. (W.) Coghill).
  Bonsall. p. 22.
  Smith N. p. 249-250.
Worship and thanks and blessing. (Charles Wesley).
  Paine. p. 464.
Yankee Doodle.
  Paine. p. 501-503.
Ye choirs of New Jerusalem. (Bishop Fulbert).
  Brown. p. 59-62.
Ye Christian heralds, go proclaim. (Mrs. Vokes (or Voke).
  Brown. p. 171-173.
Ye Christian heroes, wake to glory.
  Brown. p. 174-175.
Ye golden lamps of Heaven, farewell. (Philip Doddridge).
  Brown. p. 519.
Ye servants of God, your Master proclaim. (Charles Wesley).
  Paine. p. 740-741.
  Smith N. p. 73.
Ye simple souls that stray. (Charles Wesley).
  Paine. p. 230.
Yes, my Native Land, I love thee. (S. F. Smith).
  Paine. p. 457-459.
Yet there is room! the Lamb's bright hall. (Horatius Bonar).
  Paine. p. 305-306, 516-517, 745.
Yield not to temptation. (Horatio R. Palmer).
  Brown. p. 311.
York, (Tune).
  Paine. p. 598.
Your harps, ye trembling saints. (Augustus M. Toplady).
  Brown. p. 517-518.

Pictures To Be Used With Certain Hymns

Adoration of the Shepherds. (Adolphe William Bouguereau).
   Bonsall. p. 35.
      (Away in a manger.)
Angel. (Fra Angelico).
   Bonsall. p. 115.
      (The Doxology.)
Angel heads. (Sir Joshua Reynolds).
   Bonsall. p. 29.
      (Holy, holy, holy.)
The Angelus. (Jean Francois Millet).
   Bonsall. p. 29.
      (Now the day is over.)
Apparition to the shepherds. (Bernhard Plockhorst).
   Bonsall. p. 37.
      (It came upon the midnight clear.)
The ascension. (Gottlieb Biermann).
   Bonsall. p. 103.
      (Christ for the world we sing.)
At the home of Mary and Martha. (H. Hofmann).
   Bonsall. p. 95.
      What a friend we have in Jesus.)
The child Samuel. (James Sant).
   Bonsall. p. 27.
      (Hushed was the evening hmn.)
Christ and the fisherman. (Ernst K. G. Zimmermann).
   Bonsall. p. 65.
      (Jesus calls us, o'er the tumult.)
Christ blessing little children. (Bernhard Plockhorst).
   Bonsall. p. 47.
      (I think when I read that sweet story of old.)
The Christ child. (H. Hofmann).
   Bonsall. p. 77.
      (Fairest Lord Jesus.)

Christ the Consoler. (Ernst K. G. Zimmermann).
    Bonsall. *p.* 87.
        (Rescue the perishing, care for the dying.)
Christmas bells. (Edwin H. Blashfield).
    Bonsall. *p.* 41.
        (I heard the bells.)
Daniel's answer to the King. (Briton Riviere).
    Bonsall. *p.* 89.
        (O God, our help in ages past.)
David as a good shepherd. (Madame Bouguereau).
    Bonsall. *p.* 81.
        (Dare to be brave, dare to be true.)
Departure of the Mayflower. (Bayes).
    Bonsall. *p.* 59.
        (Faith of our fathers.)
Feeding her birds. (Jean François Millet).
    Bonsall. *p.* 19.
        (Father we thank Thee.)
The Good Shepherd. (Frederic Shields).
    Bonsall. *p.* 25.
        (Jesus, tender Shepherd, hear me.)
Head of St. Paul. (Raphael).
    Bonsall. *p.* 85.
        (Stand up, stand up for Jesus.)
Healing the sick. (Benjamin West).
    Bonsall. *p.* 49.
        (O love divine, that stooped to share.)
Holy night. (Correggio).
    Bonsall. *p.* 31.
        (Holy night, peaceful night!)
Holy women at the tomb. (Alex. Ender).
    Bonsall. *p.* 43.
        (Jesus Christ is risen to-day.)
An iceberg in the far North. (From photograph by Warren Taylor).
    Bonsall. *p.* 99.
        (From Greenland's icy mountains.)
Isaiah. (John S. Sargent).
    Bonsall. *p.* 101.
        (Hark, the voice of Jesus calling.)

Jacob's dream. (Murillo).
  Bonsall. p. 71.
    (Nearer, my God, to Thee.)
Jesus by the sea. (Alexandre Bida).
  Bonsall. p. 75.
    (Dear Lord and Father of mankind.)
John and Peter running to the tomb. (Eugene Burnard).
  Bonsall. p. 17.
    (Awake my soul, stretch every nerve.)
The last supper. (Leonardo da Vinci).
  Bonsall. p. 51.
    (Break Thou the bread of life.)
The Light of the world. (William Holman Hunt).
  Bonsall. p. 69.
    (O Jesus, Thou art standing.)
The lost sheep. (Alfred U. Soord).
  Bonsall. p. 91.
    (The King of love my Shepherd is.)
Moses. (Michelangelo).
  Bonsall. p. 113.
    (The Commandments.)
Nativity. (H. Le Rolle).
  Bonsall. p. 33.
    (Once in Royal David's City.)
"Peace, be still." (Anton Dietrich).
  Bonsall. p. 97.
    (Jesus, Saviour, pilot me.)
Peter freed by the Angel. (William Hilton).
  Bonsall. p. 67.
    (He leadeth me: Oh, blessed thought.)
Peter's denial of Christ. (Graf Harrach).
  Bonsall. p. 53.
    (In the hour of trial.)
The Prodigal Son and his father. (Martin Von Molitor).
  Bonsall. p. 73.
    (Love divine, all love excelling.)
The Puritan. (Augustus St. Gaudens).
  Bonsall. p. 61.
    (How firm a foundation.)

Rheims Cathedral.
   Bonsall. p. 55.
     (The church's one foundation.)
St. George. (Donatello).
   Bonsall. p. 83.
     (Onward, Christian soldiers.)
Shaw Memorial, Boston. (Augustus Saint Gaudens).
   Bonsall. p. 109.
     (Mine eyes have seen the glory.)
Sir Galahad. (G. F. Watts).
   Bonsall. p. 105.
     (The Son of God goes forth to war.)
Song of the lark. (Jules Adolphe Breton).
   Bonsall. p. 21.
     (When morning gilds the sky.)
The sower. (Jean François Millet).
   Bonsall. p. 23.
     (Work for the night is coming.)
Statue of Liberty, New York Harbor. (Bartholdi).
   Bonsall. p. 107.
     (My Country, 'tis of Thee.)
"Suffer the little children to come unto me." (Ottilie Roederstein).
   Bonsall. p. 57.
     (Jesus loves me.)
Victory, O Lord! (Sir John E. Millais).
   Bonsall. p. 63.
     (Who is on the Lord's side?)
Wartburg Castle.
   Bonsall. p. 93.
     (A mighty fortress is our God.)
The wise men on the way to Bethlehem. (Henry A. Harper).
   Bonsall. p. 39.
     (O little town of Bethlehem.)
Women at the sepulcher. (Adolphe William Bouguereau).
   Bonsall. p. 45.
     (The day of resurrection.)
The Yosemite.
   Bonsall. p. 111.
     (O beautiful for spacious skies.)